STUDENTS UNDER STRESS

STUDENTS UNDER STRESS

**A Study in the
Social Psychology
of Adaptation**

David Mechanic

The University of Wisconsin Press

Published 1978
The University of Wisconsin Press
Box 1379, Madison, Wisconsin 53701
The University of Wisconsin Press, Ltd.
70 Great Russell Street, London

Wisconsin edition
First printing, 1978

Originally published in 1962
by The Free Press of Glencoe,
A Division of The Macmillan Company

Printed in the United States of America
ISBN 0-299-07470-6 cloth, 0-299-7474-9 paper
LC 77-91058

To My Parents

CONTENTS

AUTHOR'S FOREWORD

THE STUDY described in this book was completed in 1960 and published in 1962. Although "stress" was already a growing concern, intellectual leadership in the description and study of adaptation to stress was dominated by psychoanalytic ideas and was understood almost exclusively in terms of the psychological defenses that were of interest to psychoanalysts and ego psychologists. Adaptation was seen as a process occurring in people's heads, with little attention paid to the actual skills individuals applied to counter adversity. The purpose of the study was to develop a better understanding of the social context of stress and the ways people under threat came to understand their situation and apply themselves to mastering it. I was particularly interested in illustrating how the social context and social interaction conditioned efforts at coping with necessary tasks and controlling emotional distress.

In the 1950s and early 1960s psychoanalytic theories of ego defense dominated the study of stress. Following the work of Freud, defense mechanisms were viewed as pathological unconscious processes that protected the individual against pain and suffering. While ego psychologists no longer viewed these defenses as necessarily pathological, the focus continued on adaptation as a protective psychological process rather than as a pattern of constructive behavior designed to deal with tasks and interpersonal challenges in the social setting.

The Freudian conception of man was a pessimistic one—repression and neurosis were inevitable consequences of the

This foreword includes material excerpted from chapter 3, "Social Structure and Personal Adaptation: Some Neglected Dimensions," by David Mechanic in *Coping and Adaptation,* edited by George V. Coelho, David A. Hamburg, and John E. Adams,© 1974 by Basic Books, Inc., Publishers, New York.

conflict between man's basic needs and the demands of the social environment. In Freud's system of thought concerning adaptation, the only concept that even remotely represented constructive response was sublimation, the transfer of libido to artistic, intellectual, and other creative efforts. In contrast, the study of *Students Under Stress* focused on constructive aspects of behavior and on the ways individuals and groups appraised situations, structured them to their own advantage when possible, and used their skills and resources to master them. People were not viewed as helpless under stress, dependent on mental tricks to protect themselves against pain and suffering. They were seen, in contrast, as active persons who could work either as individuals or cooperatively to confront challenge and, depending on their strategies and skills, reverse it.

Successful personal adaptation, as I saw it, had at least three components at the individual level. First, the person must have the capabilities and skills to deal with the social and environmental demands; for the sake of simplicity I designated these as coping capabilities. Coping involves not only the ability to react to environmental demands, but also the ability to influence and control both the demands to which one will be exposed and the pace of exposure. Second, individuals must be motivated to meet the demands that become evident in their environment. Individuals can escape anxiety and discomfort by lowering their motivation and aspirations, but there are frequently social constraints against this. As motivation increases, the consequences of failing to achieve mastery also increase, so that the level of motivation frequently becomes an important prerequisite for experiencing psychological discomfort. Third, individuals must have the ability to maintain a state of psychological equilibrium so that they can direct their energies and skills to meeting external in contrast to internal needs. Most of the psychological literature on adaptation was concerned with this third dimension—one that I referred to as defense. Although psychologists who have studied stress have viewed defense as an end in itself, it is more reasonable to see defense as a set of mechanisms that facilitate continuing performance and mastery. Defenses that may be very successful in diminishing pain and discomfort may be catastrophic for personal adaptation if they retard behavior directed toward real threats in the environment.

The fit between the social structure and environmental demands is probably the major determinant of successful social adaptation. The ability to cope with the environment depends on the efficacy of the solutions that one's culture provides, and the skills one develops are dependent on the adequacy of the preparatory institutions to which one has been exposed. To the extent that schools and informal types of preparation are inadequate to the tasks people face, social disruption and personal failure will be inevitable no matter how effective the individual's psychological capacities. Similarly, the kinds of motivation that people have and the directions in which such motivation will be channeled will depend on the incentive systems in a society—the patterns of behavior and performance that are valued and those that are condemned.

Finally, the ability of persons to maintain psychological comfort will depend not only on their intrapsychic resources, but also—and perhaps more important—on the social supports available or absent in the environment. People depend on others for justification and admiration, and few can survive without support from some segment of their fellows.

The influence of social structure is, of course, more complicated than this. The community not only defines solutions to environmental challenges, but also imposes new challenges through the social values it perpetuates. Institutionalized solutions to environmental problems must change as the problems and social values change. To the extent that preparatory and evaluative institutions in a society are fitted to the types of problems people in the society must face, most persons are likely to acquire the skills and capacities to meet life demands and challenges. With rapid technological and social change, however, institutionalized solutions to new problems are likely to lag behind, and the probability increases that a larger proportion of the population will have difficulties in accommodating to life problems. In large part, the literature on stress and coping has aided the myth that adaptation is dependent only on the ability of individuals to develop personal mastery over their environment. Increasingly, it is clear that many major stresses are not amenable to individual solutions, but depend on highly organized cooperative efforts that transcend those of any individual no matter how well developed his or her personal resources.

Although the details of *Students Under Stress* are as relevant today as they were when the observations were first made, the theories which this study was to counter are no longer dominant. The framework for studying social stress and adaptation presented here, with its emphasis on coping and constructive behavior, has increasingly been applied and elaborated on in studies of chronic disease, social development, and disaster.[1] Moreover, the ideas discussed in the context of student responses to stress have been applied in programs of intervention for changing health behavior and improving the community adjustment of mental patients. Educational efforts to assist patients to cope more adequately with life difficulties are based increasingly on a broad view of social adaptation and a specification of the skills and resources necessary to overcome particular challenges.

Although the stress field has blossomed in recent years, there still remains considerable confusion concerning its appropriate definition or the links between social and psychological conceptions of stress and biological models such as the one put forth by Hans Selye. In terms of the specific advancement of scientific knowledge, more clarity is achieved in research by limiting the issues in question to more manageable concepts such as attribution, compliance, helplessness, or anxiety. Although "stress researchers" in different disciplines have many interests in common—and benefit from knowledge of developments in related fields—their work is often better pursued by following their own paradigms than by trying to force diverse conceptions into a com-

1. G. V. Coelho, D. A. Hamburg, and J. E. Adams, *Coping and Adaptation* (New York: Basic Books, 1974); S. Levine and N. Scotch (eds.), *Social Stress* (Chicago: Aldine, 1970); A. H. Barton, *Communities in Disaster* (New York: Doubleday-Anchor, 1970).

mon rubric called "stress."[2] Despite its definitional difficulties, the stress-adaptation perspective assists in examining complex rather than more simple task behaviors, long-run dynamic responses rather than more simple or discrete responses, and challenges requiring a range of task and interpersonal skills. The study of student response to an important examination is one illustration of the power of this perspective. Other such complex situations include response to chronic disease, the loss of a loved one or a valued position through retirement, divorce and separation, and continuing exposure to noxious work or living environments. In the discussion that follows I plan to review briefly developments in stress research and emerging theoretical positions as well as to make some methodological comments. I also will examine briefly some of the educational implications of the doctoral examination experience which was the context for this particular stress study.

The Study of Stressful Life Events

The link between stress and illness has been an exciting and provocative area of sociomedical study, but it has been handicapped by the lack of methodologies that can capture the complexity of stress events in large population groups. Although such studies as the one reported here examine a stress situation and the response to it in detail, such an investigation requires a major effort to examine responses among a small sample. Only a young investigator with a great deal of time free from teaching and other professional responsibilities is likely to make the commitment that requires him to be in the field with his subjects every day.[3] (I was twenty-three years old when I did this study on a postdoctoral grant and had no other demands on my time.)

2. D. Mechanic, "Some Problems in Developing a Social Psychology of Adaptation to Stress," in J. McGrath (ed.), *Social and Psychological Factors in Stress* (New York: Holt, Rinehart and Winston, 1970), pp. 104-123.
3. J. Lofland, *Doing Social Life* (New York: Wiley-Interscience, 1976).

However much we may lament the fact, fields of study accelerate more in response to research technologies that can be easily applied than to the statement of new theoretical problems. In the stress field we have been the victim of many research technologies that were useful and interesting in their own way, but that diverted investigators from basic issues. The use of personality assessment tools, for example, frequently allowed the investigator to explain but not illuminate performance differences. Thus we learned that men achieved because they had a need for achievement, that they were prejudiced because they were authoritarian, and that they did not participate in organizations because they were alienated. This form of absorption by labeling characterized much discussion on stress, and although each of these conceptions involved an underlying theory of personality, the theory itself was either discredited or forgotten while researchers focused on various measures that they could correlate with a host of other information. An important more recent example of this tendency has been the "life events" research area.

A great deal of research has been stimulated by the development of the social readjustment rating scale, a list of life-change events, each weighted by a score indicating the expected adjustment required by the event.[4] This scale has many methodological limitations which I have discussed elsewhere,[5] but its easy application stimulated its use. The social readjustment rating scale was based on the assumption that life change itself was physiologically stressful because it called forth new psychological and behavioral routines.[6] Thus it was argued that even positive and desirable changes associated with achievement and mobility, which disrupted routine habits and modes of adaptation, took a physiological toll. Unfortunately, this was an assumption underly-

4. T. H. Holmes and R. H. Rahe, "The Social Readjustment Rating Scale," *Journal of Psychosomatic Research, 11,* 1967, 213-218.

5. D. Mechanic, "Some Problems in the Measurement of Stress and Social Readjustment," *Journal of Human Stress, 1,* 1975, 43-48.

6. T. H. Holmes and M. Masuda, "Life Change and Illness Susceptibility," in B. S. Dohrenwend and B. P. Dohrenwend (eds.), *Stressful Life Events: Their Nature and Effects* (New York: Wiley-Interscience, 1974), pp. 45-72.

ing the development of the scale rather than a proposition to be tested, and thus the correctness of the assumption was not verifiable through this body of research.

The influence of life change—both desirable and undesirable—on the occurrence of disease is an influence worth examining not only in relationship to disease patterns in general, but more important in relation to specific disease entities such as coronary heart disease and schizophrenia. The issue, however, remains unresolved, with some studies supporting the global life-change hypothesis and others contesting it.[7]

The general idea underlying the life-change hypothesis is that significant life events strain the adaptive capacities of the individual even when successful, causing a cumulative "wear and tear" on the body and, thus, greater vulnerability to disease. Whether disease actually occurs may depend on a variety of other factors including genetic disposition and exposure. Although individuals may seek change and may find successfully confronting challenges exhilarating, large and recurring change in living routines and life-style still may have a long-term negative impact on health. For example, average blood pressure in developed industrialized societies is higher than in some more stable nonliterate populations, and although it increases with age in the former societies this phenomenon is not universal.[8] Higher average blood pressure is associated with mortality from cardiovascular-renal disease and stroke. Although a faster pace may be psychologically satisfying for many people, their cardiovascular systems may not have adapted in an evolutionary sense rapidly enough to avoid damage.

A contrasting perspective in research on stress and disease focuses on psychological appraisal and on the features of social situations that threaten the physical capacity, the status, the

7. Ibid.; J. C. Gersten *et al.,* "An Evaluation of the Etiologic Role of Stressful Life-Change Events in Psychological Disorders" (unpublished paper, Columbia University School of Public Health). See also J. G. Rabkin and E. L. Struening, "Life Events, Stress, and Illness," *Science, 194,* 1976, 1013-1020.

8. J. Eyer, "Hypertension as a Disease of Modern Society," *International Journal of Health Services, 5,* 1975, 539-558.

security, and the significant interpersonal associations of those affected.[9] Within this view it is the perception of threat or loss that is critical. Many life changes pose significant threats to valued statuses and interpersonal relationships and thus contribute to bodily strain and disease.

These two positions are not necessarily incompatible. The concept of disease encompasses a wide range of individual bodily adaptations to genetic, developmental, and environmental influences. Certain positive life changes that are psychologically rewarding may contribute to particular body dysfunctions and not to others. Similarly, such negative psychological appraisals as loss, helplessness, or lack of worth may selectively affect disease occurrence. One of the problems with the "stress area" is that investigators have sought answers that are too global, an approach inconsistent with the real complexity of physiological and behavioral response. Understanding how life events interact with social-psychological, intrapsychic, and biological factors requires a specification of what events influence what illnesses under what conditions and through what processes. Such understanding requires clearer specification of life events, intervening variables, and disease indices.[10]

At a more global level there is considerable evidence that stress, however measured, increases the probability of maladjustment, behavioral disruption, social disorganization, and illness response. The more interesting, but difficult, questions are why persons exposed to the same stress situations respond differently and whether the intervening factors accounting for such variations are amenable to intervention. In *Students Under Stress* I concep-

9. S. Wolf and H. Goodell (eds.), *Harold Wolff's Stress and Disease,* 2d ed. (Springfield, Ill.: Charles Thomas, 1968); L. E. Hinkle, "The Effect of Exposure to Culture Change, Social Change, and Changes in Interpersonal Relationships on Health," in Dohrenwend and Dohrenwend, *op. cit.,* pp. 9-44; E. S. Paykel, "Life Stress and Psychiatric Disorder," in Dohrenwend and Dohrenwend, *op. cit.,* pp. 135-149.

10. D. Mechanic, "Discussion of Research Programs on Relations Between Stressful Life Events and Episodes of Physical Illness," in Dohrenwend and Dohrenwend, *op. cit.,* pp. 87-97.

tualized the experience of stress as dependent on the demands made by the stress situation in relationship to the resources of the individual to elicit the responses necessary to master them. Thus the magnitude of stress was dependent on the fit between what the situation required and what the individual was able to do. This conception is similar to the one later suggested by R. S. Lazarus, which stated that "when the balance of power favors the harm-producing stimulus, threat is increased. As the balance of power tends to favor the counterharm resources, threat is reduced."[11]

The Role of Appraisal in Stress

One of the dilemmas facing researchers in the stress field is whether to conceptualize stress as an appraisal of the individual or as an assessment of situational demands and coping resources independent of the person's perceptions. The difficulty stems from two types of observations. First, there are many persons who are extremely competent in an objective sense but who experience a great deal of distress when faced with a challenge. An example is the student who has a pattern of experiencing anxiety and a fear that he will do poorly on examinations but who always manages to do well. Second, there are persons who objectively lack appropriate skills but who have confidence and seem undaunted by failure. Thus some investigators have maintained that it is the subjective appraisal that is crucial and not the objective fact.

Most investigators study subjects' appraisals because of the difficulties in measuring what is stressful independent of such perceptions. The difficulty with such data in nonexperimental situations is that it becomes impossible to ascertain whether a relationship between appraisal and some independent variable results from the situation the respondent described or from the fact that because he is the kind of person he is he appraised the situation in a particular way.[12] It would be preferable to study the

11. R. S. Lazarus, *Psychological Stress and the Coping Process* (New York: McGraw-Hill, 1966).

12. G. Brown, "Meaning, Measurement, and Stress of Life Events," in Dohrenwend and Dohrenwend, *op. cit.,* pp. 217-243.

demands of the situation and the person's coping skills independent of subjective appraisal, but this is extraordinarily difficult to do with the methodological tools available. If we could do this, it would be possible to investigate the anomalous situations discussed earlier, independent of appraisal. Consider again the competent student who is always anxious prior to an examination. Such anxiety might be explained as a defensive device against possible failure in a situation of symbolic importance, as a means of increasing motivation for study, or as a consequence of low self-confidence in general. Similarly, the absence of evident stress in a situation in which the person objectively lacks the necessary skills may be a result of low aspirations, the low importance the person attributes to the situation, or a generalized self-confidence. These of course are not explanations in any serious sense. They are hypotheses that can be explored in a rigorous way under the proper research conditions.

In the study of life events there has been some progress in distinguishing between the independence of occurrence of a life event and the extent to which the person because of his particular attributes brings on the event. For example, that schizophrenics have a high rate of divorce tells us more about schizophrenics than about the impact of divorce on schizophrenia. Even if the study is prospective, the premorbid personality of the schizophrenic may be related to both the divorce and later problems. In a study of schizophrenia G. W. Brown and J. L. T. Birley developed the simple but ingenious idea of rating events dependent or independent of the person's behavior.[13] Thus, although the death of a sibling in an accident in another city is independent, divorce is not. They carried out the analysis separately for independent and dependent events and provided evidence that the associations found between life events and the occurrence of episodes of schizophrenia were not simply due to the patient's behavior. It has now become more common in studying life events to obtain data that allow some measurement of just how independent the event is.

13. G. W. Brown, and J. L. T. Birley, "Crises and Life Changes and the Onset of Schizophrenia," *Journal of Health and Social Behavior, 9,* 1968, 203-214.

In vacillating in my own work as to whether the study of appraisal is essential to the study of stress, I have come to an intermediate position. My present view is that stress results when the demands of a situation are greater than the individual's or group's capacity to deal comfortably with it. Such imbalances may exist in the perceptions of situations, in the objective facts, or both. When such imbalances exist objectively, they eventually affect perceptions of these events when the capacities and skills of the person are tested. The relationship between reality and perceptions, and the factors that may intervene, is an important focus of inquiry. Although subjective reactions and reports perhaps give us the best intuitive sense of what is going on, their use involves contamination of the event with the reaction to it, causing analytic difficulties. The focus on objective, independent measures of events, however, results in the loss of a great deal of important information. A reasonable compromise is to work at both levels simultaneously, insuring, however, that we do not confuse the measurement of objective events with people's perceptions and reactions.

Increasingly, the interesting question is not whether stress contributes to the occurrence of disease, but rather what factors combine with stress either to increase its impact or to mitigate its effect. Promising areas receiving a great deal of attention in the stress literature are social support, attribution, and learned helplessness.

The Role of Social Networks and Social Support

Although the stress literature often refers to group influences on adaptation to stress, such references are frequently diffuse. People relate to groups in a great variety of ways, and they may relate to the same group in different ways. Many groups define values and goals and serve as a reference point by which individuals may evaluate themselves; they may also serve to encourage persons and help allay anxiety. In addition, group organization and cooperation allow for the development of mastery through specialization of function, pooling of resources and information, and developing reciprocal help-giving relationships. The effectiveness of individuals in many spheres of action is dependent almost exclusively on the maintenance of viable forms of organization and cooperation that allow important tasks to be mastered.

Much of the confusion in the stress literature results because stress is frequently seen as a short-term single stimulus rather than as a complex set of changing conditions that have a history and a future. Individuals must respond to these conditions through time and must adapt their behavior to the changing character of the stimuli. Thus mastery of stress is not a simple repertoire, but an active process over time relating to demands that are themselves changing and that are often symbolically created by the groups within which people live and by new technologies developed by such groups. Adaptation itself creates new demands that require still further adaptations in a continuing spiral.[14]

Moreover, many demands are ambiguous and intangible; they are created out of the social fabric and social climate that exist at any time. Challenges, therefore, are a product of the transaction between people and their environment, and many of the demands are those that people have themselves created. To some extent, individuals can affect the demands they will be exposed to and the pace of exposure. They can select from alternative environments and reference groups in testing themselves. They not only respond but require others to respond to them. This complex interplay between individuals involves adaptive techniques that are infrequently referred to in the study of short-term single stressors. People pace themselves; they selectively seek information in relation to their needs for developing solutions on the one hand and protecting their "selves" on the other; they anticipate future situations and make plans that they test; they frequently select the grounds on which their adaptive struggles will take place and carefully choose appropriate spheres of action.

In *Students Under Stress* I made some preliminary efforts to delineate the role of social support and social networks in attemp-

---

14. R. Dubos, *Man Adapting* (New Haven, Conn.: Yale University Press, 1965).

ting to understand the ways students perceived examinations and coped with them. The study illustrates how the student's location in the social network affected the information available, perceptions of the exam process, and modes of preparation and reassurance. Moreover, I showed how social networks sometimes assisted instrumentally in providing information and tangible assistance and at other times in providing socioemotional release and support. Ties with social networks, however, were complex; at times the same persons who provided tangible assistance and reassurance were sources of anxiety and unfavorable social comparisons. In chapter 8 I examined the role of spouses in providing support or in contributing to the students' anxiety. Here I indicated some of the subtleties involved in providing social support. Blind reassurance was not particularly helpful. Meaningful support came from the spouse's communication of understanding of the student's situation with all its uncertainties and anxieties. Implicit in such support was the idea that the student's standing with the spouse was in no sense dependent on the examination performance.

S. Cobb has defined social support as information leading the subject to believe that he is cared for and loved, esteemed and valued, and belongs to a network of communication and mutual obligation.[15] More broadly, social support may involve nurturance, empathy, encouragement, information, material assistance, and expressions of sharedness.[16] Although social support has been measured only in a very primitive way in most empirical studies, there is evidence that it protects individuals against the adverse effects of stress.[17] Support as it is conceptualized and

15. S. Cobb, "Social Support as a Moderator of Life Stress," *Psychosomatic Medicine, 38,* 1976, 300-314.

16. R. Weiss, "Transition States and Other Stressful Situations: Their Nature and Programs for Their Management," in G. Caplan and M. Killilea (eds.), *Support Systems and Mutual Help: A Multidisciplinary Exploration* (New York: Grune and Stratton, 1976).

17. B. H. Kaplan, J. C. Cassel, and S. Gore, "Social Support and Health," *Medical Care* (Supplement), *15,* 1977, 47-58; J. Cassel, "The Contribution of the Social Environment to Host Resistance," *American Journal of Epidemiology, 104,* 1976, 107-123.

measured in these studies involves various interpersonal processes and requires greater specification and more focused inquiry. Moreover, we need a clearer understanding of the specific processes through which social support protects persons exposed to situational stressors. In some situations tangible assistance is crucial in coping; in others the knowledge that one is loved helps maintain a sense of esteem in the face of failure, seemingly mitigating the impact of the failure.

As the discussion in this book illustrates, being part of a network of communication may have value beyond the specific personal support provided. A dramatic instance of the importance of group structure in dealing with stress and danger is provided by E. Kogon in his discussion of the concentration camp.[18] He describes the ways the underground organization of inmates developed control over work assignments and their success in hiding and protecting valuable members of their group from the SS. Although the underground was not strong enough to forestall general SS directives involving mass murders, they came to influence much of the daily life in the camps. Such informal group structures develop in a great range of organizational settings, including prisons, mental hospitals, and military organizations, and help make daily life more tolerable for the people involved.[19]

Attributional Processes and Learned Helplessness

When faced with significant life-change events or particular life difficulties, people make efforts to interpret their experiences.

18. E. Kogon, *The Theory and Practice of Hell: The German Concentration Camps and the System Behind Them* (New York: Berkley Medallion Books, 1958).

19. G. Sykes, *The Society of Captives* (Princeton, N.J.: Princeton University Press, 1958); G. Sykes and S. Messinger, "The Inmate Social System," in R. A. Cloward *et al.* (eds.), *Theoretical Studies in Social Organization of the Prison* (New York: Social Science Research Council, 1960); E. Goffman, "The Underlife of a Public Institution: A Study of Ways of Making Out in a Mental Hospital," in E. Goffman, *Asylums* (New York: Doubleday, 1961), pp. 173-320; A. Cohen, *Deviance and Control* (Englewood Cliffs, N.J.: Prentice-Hall, 1966), pp. 78-80; D. Mechanic, "Sources of Power of Lower Participants in Complex Organizations," *Administrative Science Quarterly, 7,* 1962, 349-364.

The attributions they make to the causes of the event and their own responsibility vitally affect the ways they adapt to the demands of the situation and their feelings about it. People have differing notions of their efficacy in dealing with challenges and of their personal responsibility for failure when things go wrong. As the description of students' responses indicates, self-blame tends to be associated with depression, while blaming external factors is more frequently associated with anger.

The way a problem is defined can have dramatic impact on modes of coping. One example is the women's consciousness groups that have precipitated a major shift in the way many women interpret their lack of content and dissatisfactions. In the past, women who felt a sense of malaise and discontentment with the circumstances of their lives were likely to view this as a uniquely personal problem linked to their inadequacies as women, wives, and mothers. The women's movement now makes it more plausible to explain such distress as caused by existing inequalities, blocked opportunities, and exploitative role arrangements.

A related but more specific concept that has stimulated a great deal of experimental research in animals and humans is learned helplessness, a psychological state in which events are perceived as uncontrollable.[20] Laboratory research indicates that animals exposed to events they cannot control in the laboratory subsequently make no efforts to control events that are controllable. Helplessness is associated in experimental animals with a wide range of behavioral deficits, bodily damage such as ulceration, and even death. Martin Seligman, who developed the concept and with his students carried out a great deal of research exploring its effects, argues that learned helplessness in animals is analogous to human depression. More recently, he has suggested that depression in humans occurs when the individual feels helpless and attributes his situation to his own failures or lack of capacity.

We still have a great deal to learn about the developmental antecedents of a sense of personal efficacy and attributional tendencies. It is not clear, for example, why persons faced with the

20. M. E. P. Seligman, *Helplessness: On Depression, Development, and Death* (San Francisco: W. H. Freeman, 1975).

same life change or "stressor" differ in their definition as well as in their capacity to deal with it actively. As this study illustrates, past mastery and successful practice contribute to the person's sense of control and self-esteem, but this is only part of a very complex developmental picture. Some interesting clues are suggested by a study of depression in London in which women with an early loss of mother were more prone to depression when faced with significant life events.[21] Having several young children in the household made women more vulnerable to depression, although an outside job and an intimate relationship with a spouse or lover protected them from an adverse response to a "stressor." Although several small children tie the mother to the household and limit taking advantage of outside opportunities, a job may increase the person's sense of mastery and accomplishment. An intimate relationship provides reassurance of one's worth and alternate sources of gratification and personal power. Seligman has interpreted the early loss of mother as a possible instance of learned helplessness that manifests itself in later life with the occurrence of new challenges.

Further Problems in the Theory and Methodology of Stress Research

If we take the position that adaptation is anticipatory as well as reactive and that people frequently approach their environment with plans, the study of such processes takes a somewhat different direction. According to such a view, people attempt to take on tasks they feel they can handle, they actively seek information and feedback, they plan and anticipate problems, they insulate themselves against defeat in a variety of ways, they keep their options open, they distribute their commitments, they set the stage

---

21. G. W. Brown, M. N. Bhrolcháin, and T. Harris, "Social Class and Psychiatric Disturbance Among Women in an Urban Population," *Sociology, 9,* 1975, 225-254. See also G. W. Brown, T. Harris, and J. R. Copeland, "Depression and Loss," *British Journal of Psychiatry, 130,* 1977, 1-18.

for new efforts by practice and rehearsal, and they try various solutions. One cannot study such activities very effectively within an experimental mode that subjects people to specific stimuli and measures only limited reactions to these stimuli. Methodological models for successful study of such active processes of coping are undeveloped, however, and the lack of richness in experimental stress literature reflects the absence of a successful experimental technology for studying adaptive attempts over time.

The study of social adaptation could benefit substantially from a richer interaction between field studies and more precise laboratory experiments. There are obvious ethical barriers in creating stressful life circumstances, but there are many real circumstances that are amenable to study using experimental methodologies. Further, we have to develop more complex experimental models that do not restrict so closely the subject's opportunity to exercise his adaptive repertoire in dealing with laboratory situations. We must provide richer opportunities for subjects than the option of pushing one or another lever. Particularly impressive use of quasi-experimental models under natural circumstances are such investigations as S. Epstein's study of paratrooper exercises and J. K. Skipper, Jr., and R. C. Leonard's study of response to the stress of hospitalization and tonsillectomy.[22]

We still have a great deal to learn from field studies of adaptation to particular stress events over time. Such involvement requires greater emphasis on prospective studies. Because this need has been expressed many times before I will emphasize some specific considerations rather than the more general points. We must go beyond people's subjective reports of their feelings and their responses to particular stressful circumstances. Descriptions of events and responses to them are particularly dubious when

22. S. Epstein, "The Measurement of Drive and Conflict in Humans," in M. R. Jones (ed.), *Nebraska Symposium on Motivation* (Lincoln: University of Nebraska Press, 1962), pp. 127-209; J. K. Skipper, Jr., and R. C. Leonard, "Children, Stress and Hospitalization: A Field Experiment," *Journal of Health and Social Behavior, 9,* 1968, 275-287.

they are reported retrospectively because part of the process of adaptation involves the subtle restructuring of the individual's attitudinal set toward events that have taken place.[23] Successful adaptation requires changes in attitudes and perspectives that are sufficiently subtle so that the person may hardly recognize the changes. Extreme and sudden modifications of attitudes and perspectives are likely to produce new stresses, and indeed when such dramatic changes occur, this is in itself evidence of difficulties and disruptions in successful adaptation. We therefore must be suspicious of reconstructions of the past as true representations of what really took place.

At the theoretical level one of the largest tasks faced by stress researchers is the development of models that specify in a predictive sense the conditions under which one set of adaptations will develop in contrast to others. It is necessary to do more than describe the array of behaviors characteristic of persons' adaptive attempts; we must begin to specify the relative probabilities that under given circumstances one coping attempt will follow rather than another. This theoretical approach will depend on rich field studies that depict the scope of alternatives, followed by more controlled laboratory studies that attempt to determine the conditions under which one or another form of behavior follows. In short, theoretical needs require a range of methods, and if investigators do not choose to be eclectic themselves, at least some dialogue among approaches must be maintained.

The literature abounds with research and discussion of particular defenses in isolation from others. Thus we find discussions dealing with compensation (that is, the tendency to do particularly well in some areas to overcome inadequacies in others) that show no awareness of an opposing literature on status congruency (the psychological tendency to maintain one's various statuses at approximately the same level). The theory of compensation argues

23. F. Davis, *Passage Through Crisis: Polio Victims and their Families* (Indianapolis: Bobbs-Merrill, 1963); L. N. Robins, "Follow-Up Studies Investigating Childhood Disorders," in E. H. Hare and J. K. Wing (eds.), *Psychiatric Epidemiology* (London: Oxford University Press, 1970), pp. 29-68.

that people strive toward maintaining unequal levels of performance, although the theory of status congruency maintains that people strive toward maintaining equal levels of performance. Such contradictions lead to theoretical contributions by suggesting that important intervening variables have been neglected. In the example cited it is likely that people tend to compensate when a particular dimension of their status or performance is blocked or unalterable. When there is opportunity to perform in any of several spheres, however, it may be that the need for congruency is dominant.

Some Practical Implications

Some of the ideas concerning adaptation as an active stance toward mastering environmental challenges have stimulated a variety of new ways to assist people with their problems. Efforts are now made to teach people new skills in dealing with tasks and other individuals, to assert themselves in social situations, and to achieve a sense of greater personal control over their own lives. Increasingly, the value of a purely medical approach to the rehabilitation of chronic patients is being questioned as compared with social and educational models that enhance patients' behavioral repertoires and thus their ability to deal with their physical or psychological limitations, that remove barriers in the environment to their full participation, and that strengthen systems of social support.

One such example is a program entitled "Training in Community Living" in which chronic mental patients have been assigned randomly to a community program based on an educational model in contrast to a progressive but more traditional in-hospital treatment and community aftercare program.[24] In the experimental program patients participate in a

24. L. I. Stein, M. A. Test, and A. J. Marx, "Alternative to the Hospital: A Controlled Study," *American Journal of Psychiatry, 132,* 1975, 517-522; L. I. Stein, and M. A. Test, "Training in Community Living: One-Year Evaluation," *American Journal of Psychiatry, 133,* 1976, 917-918.

full schedule of daily living activities in which they are taught such simple coping skills as shopping, cooking, budgeting, using transportation, and on-the-job problem solving. Staff in the program provide a great deal of social support, promulgating a "can do" philosophy. Other efforts are made to work with families and the community to influence them to respond to patients in a manner that might promote "responsible behavior rather than reinforce maladaptive modes of coping with stress." Evaluation of the program thus far indicates considerable success in maintaining these patients in the community at a quality of performance and level of adjustment, esteem, and personal satisfaction comparable to or better than those treated in the progressive hospital situation.

In the case of treatment of chronic illness of all types, we have come to the realization that disability is as much a social definition as a physical status and that the patients' outcome depends as well on the patients' psychological state and the reactions of physicians, families, friends, and employers. By their responses these persons may either facilitate a resumption of ordinary social roles or exacerbate the patients' problems by overprotectiveness, stigmatization, or social exclusion.[25] In a study of response to coronary heart disease, for example, Laura Reif found that many such patients were defined by themselves or others as disabled despite minimal biological impairment.[26] Many of the social problems associated with handicap stem as much from physical and social arrangements in the community as from the patients' physical limitations. Frequently successful adaptation can be facilitated more by modification of social definitions and social policies than by any specific medical intervention.

25. D. Mechanic, "Illness Behavior, Social Adaptation and the Management of Illness: A Comparison of Educational and Medical Models," *The Journal of Nervous and Mental Disease, 165,* 1977, 79-87.

26. L. Reif, "Cardiacs and Normals: The Social Construction of a Disability" (Ph.D. dissertation, University of California-San Francisco, 1975).

Preliminary Examinations as an Educational Experience

In conclusion, something should be said about Ph.D. preliminary examinations, the stress situation studied in this monograph. Although these examinations served as the context rather than the focus of the monograph, some reviewers felt, depending on their perspective, that I should have done more either to defend this type of examination or to reveal its total bankruptcy. In the past seventeen years as a faculty member at Wisconsin I have seen among students and faculty more discussion and agonizing over preliminary doctoral examinations than any other issue in graduate education. Being a definite hurdle that all aspiring Ph.D.s feel anxiety about, it serves as a focal point for almost every type of debate relevant to graduate work. Although I have seen students who used this event to demonstrate their mastery and build their esteem, most students I have known, even the very best ones, have found these examinations extraordinarily stressful and frequently humiliating. Over the years, whatever confidence I may have had in the value of such examinations has become eroded, and I believe that for most students these examinations as presently constituted in most graduate departments are counterproductive, having little relevance to their future professional lives.

Most of my colleagues continue to defend these examinations with the same arguments given by the professors reported on in this monograph, and these arguments have a certain validity. The exams require students to study more broadly than they might otherwise, to organize their understanding of broad fields of knowledge, and to develop habits for concentrated effort. They serve to screen out some who may be too lazy or too disorganized, or who lack sufficient motivation to devote themselves wholeheartedly to the necessary study. In a rather perverse way such exams also test the students under stress, a form of test that prepares the student for real professional life, or so it is alleged.

Finally, if nothing else, the examinations are a test of commitment to the field, a guarantee from the student that he really cares enough to incur the costs necessary.

One major conclusion that emerges from the monograph—that there is a major difference between the ways faculty conceive of the examinations and the students' response to them—has been documented in a variety of educational contexts.[27] Although many faculty have an ideal concept of the way students should behave, students faced with the realities of passing examinations develop approaches that contain their distress and increase their probabilities of success. That such strategies may violate the expectation of achieving intellectual mastery may be upsetting for the student, but also irrelevant, when everything is at stake and the opportunities for failure are considerable. The result is that the examinations for many if not most students are just a poor representation of an intellectual challenge.

Both increased student agitation and faculty sensitivity have led many graduate departments to develop options such as completing special projects, writing papers, and publishing research studies. In fact, the department studied in this monograph developed similar options at the conclusion of the study and was influenced in this decision by my description of what was taking place. It would be a mistake to assume necessarily that providing options will eliminate anxieties. Much of the anxiety derives from students being evaluated and of the possibilities of a negative assessment. Although options may reduce some uncertain aspects of the situation and give the students some opportunity to mobilize resources in a manner more congenial to personal style, they cannot eliminate the discomfort that comes from knowing that others will be making decisions about their work that can

27. See, for example, H. Becker *et al., Boys in White: Student Culture in Medical School* (Chicago: University of Chicago Press, 1961); H. S. Becker *et al., Making the Grade: The Academic Side of College Life* (New York: John Wiley, 1968); C. D. Orth III, *Social Structure and Learning Climate: The First Year at the Harvard Business School* (Boston: Harvard Graduate School of Business Administration, Harvard University, 1963); M. Sanford, *Making It In Graduate School* (Berkeley, Calif.: Montaigne, Inc., 1976).

have an important if not critical impact on their future. Even if the student is unusually capable, there is no absolute security that the situation is under control.

Challenge and stress are inevitable in graduate school and the life beyond it. From a faculty perspective the goal is not to eliminate all stress, but to devise learning situations in which the adaptive process is consistent with the values of the profession and the achievement of competence. If this monograph contributes to the development of such options, it will have done a great deal to improve present practices.

DAVID MECHANIC

Madison, Wisconsin
October 1977

PREFACE

IN THE last fifty years the advances in understanding stress processes have come, for the most part, as the consequence of scientific knowledge of physiology, psychology, and, more recently, psychosomatic studies. There is no reason to believe that these advances are drawing to a close. More recently, however, it has become evident that one important dimension in understanding human response to stress has been sadly neglected. This is a social dimension, concerned with the tools and techniques that are provided by the social environment for dealing with threatening life situations.

Research on the nature and processes of stress reactions has been conducted with army, hospital, university, and factory populations. But while the social environment has been discussed in some of these studies, researchers have mainly emphasized the psychic and physiological mechanisms that permit defense against noxious stimulation and allow the individual to maintain his integrity and integration as a functioning personality.

Concern with the social environment as an important factor in the study of stress reactions has not been sufficiently emphasized, although such analysis is part of an important sociological tradition. W. I. Thomas argued that control of and adjustment to the environment resulted from the active manipulation of knowledge. It is the culture of the group, he wrote, that limits the power of the mind to meet crisis and to adjust. If knowledge is insufficient and material resources are scanty, an individual may find no way out of an emergency that under different conditions would be only the occasion for further progress.

This study is concerned with what W. I. Thomas would have characterized as *crisis*—or, in more modern terms, as *stress*. Here it will be argued that the groups to which a person belongs set the limits, provide the alternatives, and define the meanings to be attributed to threatening as well as nonthreatening situations. Further, it will be argued that it is the person's socially relevant groups that train the individual for legitimate and proper modes of adaptation. Adaptive devices that are unique or bizarre, or that are not recognized by the group as appropriate, can become a greater problem to the person than the threat they are designed to meet. Personal adaptation is socially formed and is related closely to the defined patterns of group activity.

In a more general sense, this study is concerned not with why an individual's functioning may become disrupted but rather with the forces that enable him to continue functioning. In short, we are concerned with the components of mental health, rather than with mental illness.

DAVID MECHANIC

Madison, Wisconsin
June 1961

1. E. H. Volkart (ed.), *Social Behavior and Personality* (New York: Social Science Research Council, 1951).

ACKNOWLEDGMENTS

MY MOST sincere thanks to the various persons who gave generously of their time to make comments and suggestions. Albert Reiss, Jr., and Edmund H. Volkart went far beyond what one might dare to expect of colleague and friend in providing detailed comments and suggestions. Samuel Fillenbaum, Lewis Froman, Jr., Robert McGinnis, Nelson Polsby, and Thomas Scheff all read a preliminary version of the manuscript and contributed in various and important ways. The author's interest in the study of stress was stimulated by David Hamburg, and many of the early ideas in approaching the problem came from his work. None of the above, of course, is in any way responsible for errors and deficiencies.

The data for this research were collected during a post-doctoral NIMH traineeship (2M-6416). The author is indebted to the National Institute of Mental Health for its support that made this book possible. The final draft of the manuscript was written during a period of research time provided by the research committee of the Graduate School of the University of Wisconsin from special funds voted by the State Legislature.

Last, but not least, the author is indebted to Alice Thompson, who typed the final manuscript, and to the students and faculty who so willingly gave of their time and patience when asked to participate in the study.

1

AN INTRODUCTION
TO THE PROBLEM

As time went on, my doubts began to increase more and more. . . . I became more and more pessimistic. I was quite sure I hadn't passed. It sort of reached the climax the day they made the decision. . . . I just couldn't go over to the building and wait for the results. So I came home and nobody was there and I sort of paced the floor a bit. Then [another student] came in and told me that he had passed and I heard that [another student friend] had passed, and they began to persuade me to call up. I wouldn't call up and I was quite positive at the time that I had failed the whole business. I was very anxious and very upset. . . . Finally, about seven o'clock I decided to call up [a faculty member] and no one answered. So I went to the building around eight o'clock. I heard that he would be there. I was really completely shook up. It took about everything I could do just to walk up the stairs and go in. I was quite convinced that I had failed, and the thing that bothered me was that I tried rationalizing everything and saying that it really wasn't that important and that I could take them over again and so forth. . . . The thing that bothered me more than anything else was I thought I had failed, but it was a question of how I could accept the failure.

THIS STUDY of an academic department at an American university is concerned with exploring and understanding how persons come to feel stress and how they deal with it. The situation selected for study is the preliminary examinations for Ph.D. candidacy—how the situation was perceived by students and how they responded to it.

The Ph.D. examination situation provides a context for the study of both the natural history of stress situations and techniques of adaptation. The term *stress* refers to the difficulties experienced by individuals as a result of perceived challenges; the term *adaptation,* to the ways in which the person deals with his situation and his feelings aroused by the situation. The primary theoretical interest of this book is to formulate the processes of adaptation to stress within the context of group relationships, which requires study of the examination process from the point of view of persons occupying various positions within the structure of the academic department studied.

The research focused on the behavior of twenty-two students, twenty of whom were taking examinations for Ph.D. candidacy.[1] But to better understand their behavior it was also necessary to talk with their spouses, faculty members, and other students at various phases in their graduate training. The research represents a case study from which we shall attempt to derive ideas and suggest implications. Whenever possible, attempts were made to test hypotheses, using short questionnaires at intervals during the time period of the investigation. Con-

---

1. When the study began twenty-two students were scheduled to take examinations in the department. Subsequently, another student signed up, and one in the original group decided against taking the examinations. We have more information about the latter than about the former. When information is available on all twenty-three students, it will be reported for the entire group.

sequently, this report contains some data that are fairly clear and conclusive and some that are more impressionistic. It is hoped that this discussion will initiate more careful study in the future of some of the hypotheses suggested. Indeed, replication, amplification, and clarification of some of the ideas here presented will require continued research in other settings.

The Stress Concept

The term *stress* has not been clearly defined in social science research. In physics and biology, where the stress concept was first used, its meaning has been fairly consistent. But when employed by social scientists, it has been used interchangeably to mean anxiety, depression, and difficulty, and hence its scope and applicability have remained elusive.

Stress was first used in a manner relevant for social science when the endocrinologist Hans Selye defined it as "the state manifested by a specific syndrome which consists of all the nonspecifically induced changes within a biologic system."[2] Various investigators since have attempted to build a bridge between the biologic stress discussed by Selye and social and psychological stress. Others have criticized the attempt to relate sociocultural stresses to biologic stresses, and some have argued that physiological stress does not refer to a phenomenon similar to these other kinds of stresses.[3] Regardless of one's position, it has

---

2. H. Selye, *The Stress of Life* (New York: McGraw-Hill Book Co., Inc., 1956), p. 54.

3. For a discussion of the objections raised, see I. L. Janis, *Psychological Stress* (New York: John Wiley and Sons, Inc., 1958), pp. 11-13. For an opposing view see Howard B. Kaplan and Samuel W. Bloom, "The Use of Sociological and Social Psychological Concepts in Physiological Research," *The Journal of Nervous and Mental Disease, 131,* 1960, 128-134.

been recognized that serious methodological difficulties do exist in building a sound bridge between the concepts of biological, psychological, and social stress. Because of the confusion in the use of *stress,* it is especially important that some of the ways in which the term has been treated in social and behavioral studies be reviewed and that the way we shall use it in this study be specified clearly.

STRESS SITUATIONS. The term *stress* has been used to refer to a situation that causes people to react in a particular way. In the biological sciences a stress situation is one where extreme changes in temperature occur, where noxious substances are injected into the body, or the like.[4] In social-behavioral studies stress has been used to characterize physical, social, and cultural conditions likely to be discomforting for most people living within a specified group. Stress situations might include battle conditions, impending surgery, rapid cultural change, a difficult but important interview, intense competition, a life crisis (such as the death of a loved one), natural disasters (floods, tornadoes, and earthquakes), acute illness or injury, frustration and failure, and so on.[5] In other words, the designation of certain circumstances as stress situations is based on an assumption: the investigator intuitively selects various aspects of the physical, social, and cultural

---

4. Selye, *op. cit.*

5. For some examples see: R. R. Grinker and J. P. Spiegel, *Men Under Stress* (New York: McGraw-Hill Book Co., Inc., 1945); Janis, *op. cit.;* I. L. Janis, *Air War and Emotional Stress* (New York: McGraw-Hill Book Co., Inc., 1951); E. Lindemann, "Modifications in the Course of Ulcerative Colitis in Relationship to Changes in Life Situations and Reaction Patterns," in Res. Publ. Assn. Nerv. Ment. Dis., *29, Life Stress and Bodily Disease* (Baltimore: Williams and Wilkins, 1950); E. H. Volkart, "Bereavement and Mental Health," in A. H. Leighton, J. Clausen, and R. N. Wilson (eds.), *Explorations in Social Psychiatry* (New York: Basic Books, 1957); and S. Liebman (ed.), *Stress Situations* (Philadelphia: J. B. Lippincott Co., 1955).

environments that he assumes are likely to lead to experiences of discomfort for most people living within some designated group, the discomfort being reflected by both social and psychological responses.

This assumption, that a stress situation, in all likelihood, will elicit specified changes in behavior, requires examination. As Basowitz and his associates[6] write, stimuli can be designated as stress regardless of the responses they may evoke. They are called stress "because of their assumed or potential effect, although we well know that in any given case the organism's adaptive threshold or previous learning may preclude any disturbance of behavior."[7] That a stress situation will, in fact, bring about specified changes in behavior serves in most cases as a plausible but usually untested assumption. It would be important to be able to differentiate stress situations by their power to induce these changes. But what criterion should one choose as defining what is stressful for *most* people? Should one regard a situation as stress if 50 per cent of the population behave in the ways specified? Or should one accept the level of 75 per cent of the population? Also, how intense a response must a situation evoke before we may legitimately call it stressful and distinguish it from other life events? Stress situations—those causing changes in behavior by discomforting individuals—should be distinguished from all other possible causes of change.

STRESS AS A RESPONSE. The term *stress* has been used to refer to emotional tensions—anxiety, fear, depression, discomfort—either reported or observed, from which it is inferred that the individual is exposed to some stress situation. At times, the inferred stimulus is called *stress*, while

---

6. H. Basowitz, H. Persky, S. J. Korchin, and R. R. Grinker, *Anxiety and Stress* (New York: McGraw-Hill Book Co., Inc., 1955).

7. *Ibid.*, p. 7.

on other occasions the behavioral symptoms (anxiety, fear, and so on) are called *stress,* or sometimes *strain.* For the sake of clarity, it is important that we specify and differentiate the environmental stimulus and the responses. Basowitz and his associates have indicated that allegedly "stressful stituations" do not always produce discomforting responses in individuals:

The training program affected individuals in a variety of ways and to different degrees, and it disturbed the entire experimental group, composed of men of varying strengths and weaknesses, in a limited manner. In addition those who were disturbed often reacted idiosyncratically with respect to the system, function, or behavior affected, the degree and the direction of the disequilibrium, and the type and amount of anxiety. Since a strictly scheduled exposure to danger and possible failure evoked such a wide variety of responses, it was apparent that stress does not conform to an a priori value judgment of what *should* happen, but can only be determined by observations of what *does* happen. In future research, therefore, we should not consider stress as *imposed* upon the organism, but as its *response* to internal or external processes which reach those threshold levels that strain its physiological and psychological integrative capacities close to or beyond their limits.[8]

An alternative to concentrating on stress situations is to deal with changes in the individual's behavior as indexed, for example, by changes in his subjective responses to his life situation, his reports of his anxieties, fears, or "state of mind." But these subjective reports pose problems of both validity and reliability. For example, to what extent are a person's reports of his feeling states correlated with states of his organism measured by physiological indices, and to what extent are his re-

---

8. *Ibid.,* pp. 288-289.

ports related to the "self" he desires to present to the investigator as well as to others?[9] A statement by one of our older respondents describing his feelings during the period prior to his exams illustrates the issue: "When people told me that I didn't look anxious, I was annoyed by the fact that they didn't see me as anxious. I didn't want to walk around like some superhuman being that was learning the stuff without suffering for it."

Both of the problems of validity noted above may be alleviated, to some extent, by utilizing other behavioral data rather than by depending totally on subjective reports. Thus, the investigator can attempt to index respondents' behavior in other ways: through his own observations, the observations and ratings of judges and observers, indices of interaction, sociometric measures, and the like. Using various techniques, he may be in a better position, therefore, to evaluate the validity of any set of observations.

In this study we will define *stress* as the discomforting responses of persons in particular situations. We shall assume that when individuals experience stress they are motivated to reduce or eliminate it. To the extent that the discomforting response cannot be easily reduced or eliminated, we may expect that it will tend to be of some severity and duration.[10] Severity of stress can be measured

---

9. For an excellent discussion of the presentation of self, see E. Goffman, *The Presentation of Self in Everyday Life* (Garden City: Doubleday Anchor, 1959). A graduate department is a fruitful context for the study of presentation of self.

10. A general classification for viewing stress situations is presented by Schwab and Pritchard, and adopted by Janis, *Psychological Stress, op. cit.,* in his study of impending surgery.

(a) Mild stresses—the effects of which last from seconds to hours: e.g., annoying insects, public appearances before a large audience, missing a train, and other such minor occurrences in daily life. (b) Moderate stresses—the effects of which last from hours to days: e.g., a period of overwork, a gastric upset, a visit of an unwelcome guest, or the temporary absence of a loved one. (c) Severe stresses—the effects of which last for weeks, months,

by the intensity of discomforting response, and its duration can be indexed by the period of time these responses persist.

We have defined stress as a discomforting response because such a definition facilitates the study of adaptation. It allows us to focus on how individuals deal with what they perceive as difficult situations and on the factors affecting their perceptions. In short, we are concerned with the kinds of definitions individuals make of their environment. It is the contention of the author that whether or not a person experiences stress will depend on the means, largely learned, that he has available to deal with his life situation. Thus, the degree to which a person is able to avoid discomfort will depend on his abilities and capacities, the skills and limitations provided by group traditions and practices, the means made available to him by his social environment through learning experiences, and the norms which define when and how he may utilize these means. Thus, stress is likely to become evident when the individual perceives these means as lacking or insufficient, or when they actually do become so.

Examples of group differences in dealing with life situations have demonstrated the importance of social definitions for the study of stress. Volkart,[11] for example, in his cross-cultural studies of bereavement, has pointed

---

or even years: e.g., prolonged separation from one's family, death of a close one, drastic financial losses, illnesses, or surgical operations.

The classification as presented obviously confuses two dimensions—duration and intensity. The stress resulting from the visit of an unwelcome guest will depend both on how unwelcome he is and how long he remains. In prolonged separation from one's family, stress will depend upon how close a person feels to his family and other available alternatives, as well as the period of separation. Thus, to confuse the dimensions of duration and intensity, although they often are highly correlated, is to confound the clarity necessary in the analysis of stress situations.

11. Volkart, *op. cit.*

out that individuals usually experience discomfort of great severity and duration at a loss of a spouse or relative in groups where the deceased is defined as unique. In groups where emphasis is placed not on the uniqueness of the individual but on a replaceable pattern of reciprocal obligations, substitution can occur with lesser difficulty and adjustment to the death of a loved one can be accomplished more easily. Grinker and Spiegel also have pointed out the importance of the group and its resources in dealing with stress.

The impersonal threat of injury from the enemy, affecting all alike, produces a high degree of cohesion so that personal attachments throughout the unit become intensified. Friendships are easily made by those who might never have been compatible at home, and are cemented under fire. Out of the mutually shared hardships and dangers are born an altruism and generosity that transcend ordinary individual selfish interests. . . . It is an interesting fact that, although the members of combat crews are thrown together only by chance, they rapidly become united to each other by the strongest bonds while in combat. The character of these bonds is of the greatest significance in determining their ability to withstand the stresses of the combat situation.[12]

The importance of group resources in patterning response may be illustrated by a hypothetical example. If we examine a situation where a boat capsizes, it will appear obvious that nonswimmers are more likely to be distressed by this event than persons who can swim. To the extent that a person is an excellent swimmer, or if he has come prepared with a life jacket, the discomfort he will experience in the same situation will probably be less. Learning to swim may be regarded as a socially learned ability, and a life jacket may be regarded as a

---

12. Grinker and Spiegel, *op. cit.*, pp. 21-22.

culturally acquired instrument. If a person cannot utilize these means—or substitutes for them, such as holding on to the boat—his position is precarious. Thus, whether a person will experience stress in this situation is dependent on the means he can manipulate in the situation. This oversimplified example also illustrates another aspect of adaptation to life situations—the need for the individual to maintain sufficient control over his feelings and emotions to behave rationally in the situation. Thus, the nonswimmer must control his "panic" sufficiently to be able to recognize the alternatives open to him. This is equally true of the swimmer who must gauge whether it is wiser to hold on to the overturned boat and rest or, perhaps, to attempt a long and arduous swim to safety.

The preceding discussion highlights the importance of social and cultural means for dealing with life situations. However, since the reversibility of stress has received so little attention in earlier discussions, some further comments are necessary.

The term *reversibility* refers to the individual's successful and active mastery of a situation and to the mastery of the feelings he experiences that have been aroused by the situation. In brief, reversibility is an active form of adaptation or adjustment, dependent on the availability of personal, social, and cultural means. The severity of stress and its duration are related to the individual's capacity or that of his group to reverse it. Therefore, to understand stress we must understand the means available to deal with the situation that has elicited the discomfort and the ability of the person or group to acquire and effectively use these means. To the extent that an individual acquires the tools capable of dealing with difficult life situations, that which in some circumstances might be a threatening situation, can become routine and ordinary.

The foregoing suggests that the study of stress and adaptation can be enhanced through an investigation of how adaptive means are learned, used, and discarded. It is useful from both a theoretical and practical point of view to attempt to understand how the individual learns to eliminate stress through functional habits and attitudes. In short, while the ability to deal with stress situations may be in some cases highly personal, it is in other ways highly structured. For this reason the means available to a person, a group, or both, for dealing with stress, the modes of transmission of these means, and the group factors affecting the definition of what constitutes threat will require analysis. Before viewing these issues, however, it is essential that the research context be described clearly.

2

THE RESEARCH CONTEXT

WITHIN THE UNIVERSITY department studied attention has been centered mainly on two groups: faculty and graduate students. Faculty positions are explicitly stratified into the usual professorial ranks. And, as will become evident as the description of this study develops, the esteem and recognition accorded by students to individuals holding these ranks varied greatly.

Unlike that of faculty, the graduate student status is not clearly demarcated. There is, however, a recognizable stratification in part officially structured and informally determined. And since student status does have considerable bearing on behavior within a department, a discussion of factors influencing student status is important. The most obvious of the distinctions between types of graduate students that has relevance for the department studied is that between old and new students—a distinction referring to the length of time the person has spent as a graduate. In a certain sense, the old student has withstood the early graduate challenges and often regards himself as more a part of the surroundings and more worthy of faculty attention than the student who has recently arrived. As a teaching or research assistant, he is more likely to know the "ropes," and this knowledge, as well as his graduate progress, may serve as an implicit claim for attention. Yet, as the performance of students is highly variable, the potential and ability possessed by the new student may accord him such sufficient personal esteem as to more than make up for the small differences in prestige between the younger and older student.[1] The new student also represents an unknown quality, and, if he has been highly recommended to graduate school by reputable persons, or can produce cues that demonstrate his potential, he is likely to receive considerable attention from faculty members who are interested in learning the limits of his abilities and knowledge. Thus, while the distinction between the "new" and the "old" student may have meaning in student perceptions, this pecking order may be attended to less seriously by the faculty.

The student's status as "old" or "new" is also likely to influence the communication in which he takes part. While there is considerable communication between old and new students, communication and competition are most likely to occur within the group with whom the student enters graduate school, in part, as a result of similar course-loads, high opportunity for everyday interaction, and common interests and problems. The "old" and "new" dichotomy is also a clue to the knowledge the stu-

---

1. Following the usage of K. Davis, *Human Society* (New York: The Macmillan Co., 1949), *prestige* refers to the rank of the position, *esteem* to the performance of occupants holding a position.

dent has about the inner workings of the department. Whereas the "old" student has already learned his way around, the new man, to use an old student's phrase, "is wet behind the ears." And, at least in the beginning, the older student serves as the source of information for the newcomer, who is likely to seek advice from the more experienced men about courses, professors, gimmicks, and the like. To use a well-worn phrase, the department has something of a culture and a tradition, part of which is communicated from one student generation to the next.

The student evaluates his progress by his grades, faculty cues, and his relative capabilities to others in his year-group. A clearer indication of where he stands in comparison to others in his group is based on the fellowship or assistantship he receives. Although the hierarchy of fellowships, scholarships, and assistantships is not formally announced, students do report distinctions among the distributed awards and perceive these as indications of where they stand in faculty esteem. They also use the rewards others receive as a basis for judging them.[2]

While the distinctions between the "old" and "new" student may be somewhat blurred, they are clearer between the student who has passed the preliminary examinations and the one who has not. The examinations demarcate two graded positions, that of *candidate* and that of *precandidate*. Whereas the future security of the precandidate is unclear and uncertain in his own mind,

---

2. The rewards received by the graduate student may be treated as an assignment to positions other than that of student. For example, the graduate student may also hold an instructorship within his department. For our purposes, however, it will be sufficient to treat positions of less than full faculty rank as rewards, and not concern ourselves to any extent with the duties and rights of these positions which are secondary to our interest in stress and adaptation.

the status of candidate includes an acceptance and recognition by faculty and students that in all probability he will earn the doctorate. The examinations thus serve as a *rite-de-passage* through which the successful student may acquire the *candidate* status. As one candidate reported:

After you pass the examinations, there's a feeling of acceptance. There's a feeling that you're finally accepted and respected by the staff, and also that you are going to get your Ph.D. which is really a positive thing that comes out of these things. And up until that time, you are sort of a trainee and you don't have your stripes yet. And after you pass these, you have a feeling of accomplishment and a feeling that they are really interested and concerned with getting you through.

Like the draftee, however, the student may not view the process with such equanimity, although he may accurately perceive the steps in the Ph.D. process. The student approaching the examination experience or the student who has failed to pass successfully on prior attempts is more likely to feel hostile toward the examiners. As one student who was repeating the examinations indicated:

They have a tendency to shit all over you until they feel like accepting you, and then you are supposed to turn and love them because *now* you are one of the boys. You passed the hazing period and you are a member of the fraternity and you are supposed to be full of camaraderie, good fellowship, and so forth. I don't like this sort of procedure. . . . I don't know to what degree it is necessary or not, but I don't like it.

The foregoing suggests that the preliminary examination situation is a source of considerable stress in the department studied. As our description of the department unfolds, it will become clear why the student is greatly involved. We have already suggested its structural significance—it is the determining point of whether the individual will move to a higher status within the department, a position which to a large extent may determine his future.

The Stress Situation Studied

The group under study consisted of twenty students taking departmental written examinations for the Ph.D. degree and two students taking departmental written examinations for the M.A. degree. In the department studied, the Ph.D. examinations presented the major obstacle to departmental acceptance, and the student who passed felt some assurance that he would eventually receive the Ph.D. degree.

The examinations in the department covered nine different areas and required eighteen hours. Three of the areas were mandatory for all students and made up the core curriculum. Completion of the examinations took approximately a week, and for most students the intensive studying period prior to examinations usually covered a span of a few months. After the examinations, approximately two weeks passed before the student was informed of his outcome.

This examination situation provided an excellent context for the study of stress situations and adaptation. The examinations supplied discomfort of some intensity for most students as will be demonstrated; the studying and examination periods covered a fairly long duration; and this context furnished a source for careful study of the reversibility dimension of stress, the extent to which socially defined means are developed and utilized in adaptation to stress.

Method of Study

Three months prior to examinations, the investigator approached all students scheduled to take examinations. Each was asked to participate in weekly interviews with him for the following four months. Nineteen of the twenty-two students consented to participate in the study. The three students who refused gave time pressures as their reason. Individual interviews were held with the nineteen participating students at weekly and bimonthly periods. On the average each student was interviewed approximately ten times, including before and after examination interviews. Also on several occasions sociometric and other quantitative data were elicited from these students.

Approximately four weeks prior to examinations, students were asked to complete a comprehensive questionnaire covering their examination experiences. This questionnaire, constructed on the basis of the hypotheses developed as a result of the early interviews, was responded to by all of the twenty-two students taking examinations. The spouses of the students taking the examinations also were interviewed so that family influences and effects of the examinations on familial interaction could be evaluated.

In addition, a shorter but similar questionnaire to the one completed by the students was administered to faculty members in the department so as to allow us to study faculty perceptions of their interaction with graduate students, as well as their own attitudes toward the examinations. Also, a number of faculty members were interviewed both formally and informally on several occasions. Interaction among department members was frequently observed informally and the researcher also attended the faculty meeting concerned with the examinations.

Approximately four weeks following examinations, short questionnaires were sent both to the group under study and to a number of other students in the department. This questionnaire investigated post-examination attitudes of those who took them and explored how other students in the department viewed the examination process. Other oportunities to elicit student opinion were utilized; and data were obtained by informal discussion, lunches, informal visiting, and participation in department activities.

The Unit of Study

This is a study of graduate students in their various role-sets: in relationship to other students, faculty members, and family. In viewing the various role-sets the student assumes in relation to one major life-event (the doctoral preliminary examinations), it is hoped that the social-psychological and sociological implications for adaptation will become clearer. The student's behavior relative to the situation depends, in part, upon his position in the department and the organization of his various role-sets. The attitudes and demands of his wife and the manner in which he is viewed by other students and faculty affect his definition of the situation and his ability to deal adequately with it. By considering the student's relationships with other students, the way he adapts may be amplified not only in relation to the task or challenge but also in regard to how the demands of various persons ease or exacerbate the challenge of the situation.

The sample or situation being studied may be viewed in various ways. From one point of view, the students under study represented a group, perhaps in some ways representative of later groups of students who will function in the same department under similar situations, assuming the department maintains its admission policies and procedures; or the department may be representative, in some measure, of graduate departments at other universities that have a similar structure and tradition. This sample, however, was in no way drawn to be representative of graduate students in general, or even of the department studied, since to some extent the department does modify its procedures from year to year. Nor are the traditions and procedures of the department studied necessarily similar to other departments in the same academic area at other universities, or to other departments at the same university. For our purposes, the department can be viewed best as a case used for the purpose of studying processes of adaptation during a particular time interval. Since the major purpose of the study was to develop, not test, hypotheses, the selection of the sample has not received the attention that would be necessary in a more rigorous research design.

The Students' Definitions of the Situation

Examinations are defined as important by students since they represent a point of passage from the less prestigeful student status of precandidate to the more valued status of candidate. And the concern the student experiences in going through the examination process often will depend on the perceived importance of this status shift for his future life experiences and the degree to which he views his performance as reflecting upon his worth as a person. Before presenting the findings concerning adaptation, it is important first to describe the personal meanings that various students attribute to these examinations.

Formally speaking, the student taking examinations can have at least four possible outcomes. He may fail the examinations completely; he may pass the examinations on the Master's level but be terminated; he may pass on the Master's level but may be required to retake the examinations for the Ph.D.; or he may pass at the Ph.D. level and complete fully his written examination obligations. The result a student learns to expect depends on his experience in the graduate program and what he sees as the usual outcome of persons around him. What the student aims for on these examinations, therefore, is established by bringing his level of aspiration into line with the past experience of others he has known who are perceived as having abilities similar to his own as well as the apparent expectations of other students in his group.

The formal possibilities are not necessarily the "real" ones. Students are unlikely to be "flunked out" of the program without a Master's degree after two years of work; at least no such case was discovered in this department. A more realistic possibility is the terminal Master's, but students consider it more in the realm of a possible than likely outcome. Even following failure, the student is usually allowed another attempt to pass the examinations if he so desires. The latter two formal possibilities—Master's pass but retake for the Ph.D. (or failure at the Ph.D. level for those who already have Masters' degrees) and the Ph.D. pass—are the most common outcomes. Even for the student taking examinations for the first time, a major source of stress lies in the desire to pass on the Ph.D. level and, therefore, to avoid repeating the arduous study period and a week of examinations. Also at stake is the student's own esteem vis-à-vis others in his group should his close associates pass the examinations while he fails. Considering the aspirations of the particular group under study, failure to pass at the Ph.D. level was defined as a defeat. This general statement, however, does little justice to the complex factors that determine estimates of what constitutes a good and a bad result. At this point it is necessary that we attempt to specify further some of the factors that distinguish students in their views of the meaning of failure.

The Students Studied

Six of the students under study had taken the examinations on a previous occasion. Some of these also had had graduate training at other institutions. Students repeating the examinations see them as less useful educationally and more bothersome than do the second-year students. Moreover, these students are also disturbed by the realization that they are making what may be their last try. Should they fail, it is unlikely that they will be allowed another attempt.

Three of the students studied, although they had not taken the examinations on previous occasions, had entered the department with prior graduate work and the Master's degree. For these students the Master's pass represented a clear failure since they could not earn what they already had. In their case the necessity of passing at the Ph.D. level was more pressing than in the case of second-year students.

Two of the students in the group were studying for terminal Master's degrees and had no ambitions for the Ph.D. This pair experienced considerably less stress than did the group as a whole.

The remaining twelve students were all in their second year of graduate study. For them, passing at the Ph.D. level was less clearly mandatory. The degree of stress experienced by these students did vary, however, and the variation was contingent on their involvement in the situation.

Involvement in the Situation

After two years of graduate study the student has already invested considerable time, money, and effort in his training. By this time most students have developed strong feelings of involvement and associate socially with others similarly involved. Since friendships are usually built with others in the same or similar fields as a result of propinquity and common interests, students reinforce each other's involvements and in part accord esteem to others on the basis of their proficiency as students.

It is likely, therefore, that the student's self-esteem, as well as the esteem that others have for him, will be largely associated with his performance as a student and with the faculty's opinion of him. As one student described the examinations: "These things serve a very personal function for you. Your whole adequacy depends on them and maybe this is one of the crucial things. I remember that I felt that my whole feelings of self-esteem rested on these things. . . . I couldn't fail because they were the biggest things."

Failure in the case of students who have or expect children is viewed as extremely serious. Moreover, the married student, as compared with the single one, usually has additional financial problems and there is more pressure on him to enter the world of work. One married student commented: "I would like to know that I'm going to get through it all right so we can plan ahead. Now that we have a baby coming along, it is going to make me a little more desiresome of getting through these things." The unmarried student can take a different attitude toward the examinations:

I suppose if I was married and had three children I would feel like this was a much more stressful situation because of the responsibilities. I don't feel, if I don't get the degree here, that it's going to be a great tragedy. It isn't anything to laugh about and it certainly isn't nice. But it isn't like my wife and kids are going to starve because of it.

From a practical point of view the student realizes that the Ph.D. represents a union card for full entrance into the professional world. The more desirable jobs and income opportunities are dependent in large part on acquisition of the Ph.D. Thus, the apparent necessity of the academic degree for college teaching at a major university is clear to the student, as is the considerable economic importance of the Ph.D.

I was talking about the possible outcomes. . . . I talked to [another student] about them. He said that if he did not pass he might go teach at a junior college or something. . . . I said I couldn't look at it that way. . . . I don't know exactly how I can accept the thing if I do not pass. . . . There's too much involved. I've spent too much time. There's lots of other reasons. It's not that I think a Ph.D. is so great. . . . The point is that I have spent this time, and if I do not accomplish anything with all this, it will be a difficult thing.

We have already made some allusions to the fear the student experienced as to losing the esteem of others—family, friends, and fellow students—for a person's own esteem is dependent upon how those significant to him feel about him. This was reflected in a comment by a student who had failed the examinations on an earlier occasion, and who had been a graduate student for a number of years: "The whole thing has made a joke out of me. . . . I think people compare themselves with me around here to make themselves feel better. And when I go back home, people think I'm sort of a jerk, going to school for so many years. . . . I don't think this can be immediately erased."

Thus the examinations represent not only an academic challenge but also a challenge to self-esteem, to the role as husband and father, and to the future role as a professional. As one of the students put it: "It's a real challenge. It's one of the greatest challenges I have ever been faced with. I will really feel left out if I don't make it. . . . It's real important. It's the most important thing I've ever come up against. It's either attaining what I've been going for, or not getting there."

3

THE DEPARTMENT AS A
COMMUNICATION SYSTEM

UNDERSTANDING THE MANNER in which students dealt with the examination situation requires a careful investigation of the way in which students and faculty communicated with one another within the department and of the factors affecting such communication. The students did not react uniformly to the situational threat they experienced, and the differences in behavior that were observed cannot be fully explained on the basis of personal factors. The form of communication processes within the department had a bearing on student reactions, and consideration was required of the influences of physical location and group relationships.

The student's office location was an important factor influencing with whom he communicated and his opportunities for extensive interaction concerning examinations. In general, students occupying offices next to one another or those sharing offices were more likely to communicate with one another than with students located elsewhere. The twenty-three students studied were located in five buildings scattered throughout the campus. Most of them, however, had offices in the building where the department had its main office. We shall refer to this building as the *Central Building*. Of the fifteen students who had offices in the Central Building, seven spent almost all of their time there, while the other eight divided their studying time between home and office. Most of the student offices were clustered together on the first and second floors of the Central Building.

Of the remaining eight students, four were located together in a second building, a considerable distance from the Central Building. Because this group of four students was isolated physically from the Central Building, we shall refer to them as *semi-isolates*. The remaining four students, located in three other buildings where various research projects and operations were housed, shall be designated as *physical isolates*. Table 1 shows the distribution of students and their areas of study.

Table 1—Students' Professional Specialty and Physical Location

Students' Physical Location	SPECIALTY			
	1	2	3	4
Located in Central Building (N-15)	14	—	—	1*
Physical semi-isolates (N-4)	—	3	1	—
Physical isolates (N-4)	2	—	2	—

*This student's office was isolated within the building.

As Table 1 shows, student location is contingent to a large extent on area of professional specialization. Of the fifteen students in the Central Building all but one were studying the same specialty, and he was physically isolated from the others. Ten of the fifteen students in the Central Building were second-year students with no previous graduate training; two had entered with the second-year group but already held the Master's degree from another university. Of the remaining three students in the Central Building, two had failed to pass the Ph.D. examinations in the department on earlier attempts (one of these also having had earlier graduate experience at another university) and one had recently come to the university as a transfer student with the Master's degree.

Three of the four physical semi-isolates had failed previously to pass the preliminary examinations at the Ph.D. level, while the fourth was a second-year student with no prior graduate experience. Of the four physical isolates, one had failed to pass the department examinations on a prior occasion; the second was a member of another department, working on a terminal Master's within the department; and the two remaining students were in their second year, although one of these had spent the early part of his first year in another academic department of the university.

Figure 1 shows the sociometric pattern of student communication as to examinations. A double black line between students shows a situation where both students reported a great deal of interaction concerning examinations with each other. A broken black line indicates that one student reported a great deal of interaction about examinations with the other student, while the second student reported only a fair amount of communication. The broken line shows direction—when the arrow faces a person, it indicates that he is the one who made the lower estimate. A single black line indicates that both students reported a fair amount of interaction concerning examinations.

As the reader can see from Figure 1, physical isolation and communication isolation do go together. Intense communication about examinations was negligible between students outside the Central Building and the group within. A subsystem of communication may develop within a building as in building four. But the size of the communication link formed is likely to be influenced by the physical distance separating this link with other links in the department and the size of this subgroup.

It is essential to remember that Figure 1 reflects only very frequent or fairly frequent lines of communication. Indeed, all students did communicate from time to time with persons with whom they were not linked on the figure. The figure merely illustrates the more usual lines of communication. Students also communicated with other students, young and old, who were not taking examinations. Those who were physically isolated from the main stream of communication would discuss examinations with anyone easily accessible, sometimes with students in other departments whose offices were close to their own. Thus, interaction does seem to be influenced substantially by propinquity.

In Figure 1 the reader can see two cliques of intense interaction concerning examinations linked by student nine. The clique of most intense communication included students 9, 10, 11, and 21. These students, who spent a major portion of their time in the Central Building, did almost all of their studying there. All four had entered the department at the same time, although one member of the group prior to this already held the Master's degree. The second main clique, including students 9, 13, 14, 15, and 16, all shared or occupied offices in close proximity.

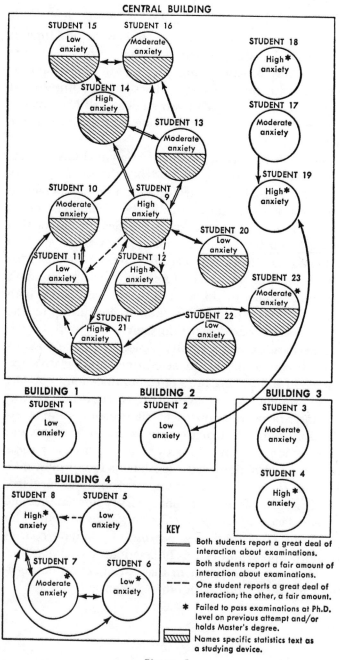

CENTRAL BUILDING

STUDENT 15 — Low anxiety
STUDENT 16 — Moderate anxiety
STUDENT 14 — High anxiety
STUDENT 13 — Moderate anxiety
STUDENT 18 — High* anxiety
STUDENT 17 — Moderate anxiety
STUDENT 19 — High* anxiety
STUDENT 10 — Moderate anxiety
STUDENT 9 — High anxiety
STUDENT 20 — Low anxiety
STUDENT 11 — Low anxiety
STUDENT 12 — High* anxiety
STUDENT 23 — Moderate* anxiety
STUDENT 21 — High* anxiety
STUDENT 22 — Low anxiety

BUILDING 1
STUDENT 1 — Low anxiety

BUILDING 2
STUDENT 2 — Low anxiety

BUILDING 3
STUDENT 3 — Moderate anxiety
STUDENT 4 — High* anxiety

BUILDING 4
STUDENT 8 — High* anxiety
STUDENT 5 — Low anxiety
STUDENT 7 — Moderate anxiety
STUDENT 6 — Low* anxiety

KEY

═══ Both students report a great deal of interaction about examinations.

───── Both students report a fair amount of interaction about examinations.

- - - - One student reports a great deal of interaction; the other, a fair amount.

* Failed to pass examinations at Ph.D. level on previous attempt and/or holds Master's degree.

▨ Names specific statistics text as a studying device.

Figure 1

The students in this group spent somewhat less time at the Central Building which probably accounts for the somewhat less intense communication in this clique as compared with the first clique described. In this second group, who also were second-year students, all had entered graduate school together at the same time as those in the first group.

The main centers of communication included primarily second-year students, all studying the same specialty within the department. Their intense rate of interaction about examinations can probably be accounted for in part by the more frequent opportunities for interaction brought about by taking the same courses, by friendships developing as a result of everyday interaction, and by common everyday interests. Moreover, their similar status as graduate students, different in some sense from both older and younger students, facilitated some group feeling and increased association within their own group.

Since location and specialty choices are closely associated, it becomes difficult to determine their relative importance in influencing rates of communication. The fact that all students taking examinations, regardless of specialty interest, were required to take three core area examinations indicates that to some extent all students did have common concerns. Moreover, it was precisely these core area examinations that the students found most difficult, and to which their main attention was devoted. Thus, it seems that location, not specialty interest, became the main factor affecting interaction. Since students who studied the same specialties because of common courses had more opportunities for interaction, a common specialty does seem important in that it can condition possibilities for interaction with other students.

Physical Location
and Acquaintanceship

Approximately eight weeks prior to examinations, students were provided with a list of all those scheduled to take examinations and were asked to indicate which of these students they did not know. Eleven of the twenty-two students were named three or more times. Most frequently named were the three physical isolates on whom we had data. Of the four semi-isolates, three were named more than three times. Of the remaining fourteen students, only five were named three or more times (see Table 2).

Table 2—Physical Location and the Extent to Which Students Could Not Be Recognized by Other Students

Physical Location	Mean Number of Times Student in Group Could not be Recognized by Others Taking Examinations
Isolates (N-3)	9.3
Semi-isolates (N-4)	3.0
Nonisolates (N-15)	2.1

Table 3—Physical Location and Communication

Physical Location	Mean Number of Persons Communicating with Members of Each Group
Isolates (N-3)	4.0
Semi-isolates (N-4)	5.5
Nonisolates (N-15)	12.4

If all interaction among the student group, casual as well as intense, was taken into account, would there be a relationship between physical location and communication? Each student was asked to indicate how much he had discussed examinations with other members of the student group. A score then was assigned to each student, indicating how many students reported that they had communicated with him to any degree about examinations. As an examination of Table 3 shows, the extent of communication among students varied by physical location.

Physical Location of Faculty
and Student Communication with Faculty

The extent of student-faculty communication concerning examinations was found to depend in part on the physical location of offices of faculty. The more easily accessible the faculty member to student location, the more likely they were frequently contacted concerning examinations. Students communicated most often with their advisors and other professors located in the same building in which they themselves were located. Since most of the students had offices in the Central Building, faculty located in the Central Building should have had the highest rates of communication about examinations with students. Of the faculty members, only ten were located in the Central Building. And these professors, regardless of area of interest, were best known by the student group. Both groups of faculty—those in the Central Building and those located outside—represented varying specialty interests, and, in some respects, the faculty outside the Central Building were more similar in interests to a majority of students than were those located in the Central Building. Examination of Table 4 will show that the extent to which students recognized faculty members depended in part upon the physical location of faculty. Since faculty in the Central Building tended to be of higher rank, it might be suspected that the effect observed was attributable to differences in rank. Table 5 takes rank into consideration.

Table 4—Physical Location of Faculty and Student Recognition of Them

Physical Location of Faculty	Mean Number of Students Who Could not Recognize Faculty Members in Group
Located in Central Building (N-10)	1.5
Located outside Central Building (N-10)	6.2

Table 5—Physical Location, Rank of Faculty, and Student Recognition of Them

Location	Mean Number of Students Who Could not Recognize Faculty Members in Group
Located in the Central Building	
Tenure professors (N-6)	1.0
Nontenure professors (N-4)	2.3
Located outside Central Building	
Tenure professors (N-2)	3.0
Nontenure professors (N-8)	7.0

Location seems to have been an important factor in the recognition of both lower-ranking faculty and tenure faculty. Regardless of rank, professors located in more accessible offices were better known and more easily recognized by students. Also, tenure faculty were more easily recognized than nontenure faculty, probably because they played a more important part in training graduate students. If our hypothesis is correct, tenure faculty should in fact play a more important role than nontenure faculty in training graduate students. Students participating in the study then were given a listing of faculty members and were asked to indicate which of the professors they had either taken courses with or worked with. Table 6 confirmed the expectation that tenure faculty do play the major role in training graduate students.

Two of the nontenure professors in the Central Building were relatively recent arrivals. On the average, the

**Table 6—Physical Location of Faculty, Professorial Rank, and
Working with Graduate Students**

Physical Location	Mean Number of Students Who Had not Taken Courses With or Worked With Professors in Group
Central Building	
Tenure professors (N-6)	6.7
Nontenure professors (N-4)	11.5
Outside Central Building	
Tenure professors (N-2)	8.5
Nontenure professors (N-8)	13.4

nontenure professors who had been in the department
for a longer period had worked with twice as many graduate students as had the more newly arrived nontenure
professors.

The Communication System
and Adaptation

The information that students have concerning examinations and the adaptive devices they use are contingent on a number of complex factors. One such factor is
the organization of student communication, which often
may determine the information the student receives and
the opinions he holds regarding the examination process.
Furthermore, the student seeks social support for the
comforting attitudes he develops relating to examinations,
and checks out information he himself is dubious about.
In a sense the communication structure is a means of air-
ing attitudes, favorable and unfavorable cognitions, devices for preparation, and so on regarding the examination
process. At this point it is sufficient to notice that the attitudes and opinions that students have about examinations,
and their means for dealing with them, were contingent

in part upon their location in the student communication structure.

Because it would be burdensome to analyze how all information is diffused through this complicated structure, a few examples will be given to illustrate how diffusion occurs.

A number of months previous to examinations, one of the students ordered a newly-published statistics text. As we will show later, students are very sensitive to the reading of other students. The book was described as clear and lucid, and was aimed at the nonmathematically sophisticated reader. Some of the students noticed this text on the desk of the individual who had purchased it. And, as the student who had bought the book spoke of it enthusiastically, information about it soon began to diffuse throughout the student communication structure. It was reported that this evaluation had been legitimized by a remark made by an important member of the department to the effect that this was an excellent statistics text. One student described why he decided to read this text: "A couple of people started talking about it and I looked at it. [An influential faculty member] mentioned one day that it was a great book. And it's just a book that's easy to read and yet it seems fairly complete."

Approximately three weeks prior to examinations, students were asked to indicate the three books or articles that they thought most important in each of their areas. In the Central Building where there was a large chain of communicators, including eleven persons (see Figure 1), all eleven indicated the statistics text as one of their three listings in the statistics area. Of the remaining eleven students, only one listed the text as one of his selections in this particular area.

Of the students who read this statistics text some were disappointed. The idea that others had found the book helpful was disturbing, especially for those who found the book confusing. One way of dealing with this discomfort was to find others who had had a similar experience and in this way to validate socially one's own experience with the text. Some evidence that this had occurred came from remarks made by a student on consecutive weeks:

I read [the statistics text]. . . . I finished it in fairly short order because I didn't find it to be very helpful. It was more confusing than anything else because of his unique approach to statistics. I do have some grasp of what is involved in analysis of variance and correlation, and I guess most of the common statistics, and his way of looking at it, was different from the approach that I had learned. So I felt that I didn't really want to concentrate on this too much. I was a little disappointed because I hoped it would suffice as preparation for the statistics section, but it won't. I'll have to go back to a more elementary book.

A week later this student found some social support for his evaluation of the book:

I guess I talked about the statistics section of the examination with [another student]. His reaction to [the statistics text] was pretty much my reaction—that it wasn't a very lucidly written book. The derivations and explanations were quite different from anything we had ever seen before. He had evidently counted pretty heavily on this book to carry him through statistics and was pretty upset about this.

The student making this report derived considerable comfort from telling the investigator that the other student had been upset that the text had not sufficed as preparation for the statistics area. At this point it is interesting to note (since it happens frequently) that when the student reports his own feelings, he describes them as "a little disappointed" and tends to use negating adjectives in his descriptions, thus minimizing his own distress. In describing the feelings of other students who have had a similar reaction, however, he will refer to this as "pretty upset," and usually will draw these descriptions with supporting adjectives, thus emphasizing the other student's distress. In a sense, the discussion here is a preview of an area we will discuss later at great length—the manner in which students utilize favorable social comparison as a defensive technique.

Most information, whether of an academic or emotional content, does not diffuse throughout the student group as widely as the information concerning this statistics text. Rather, information and reassurances are communicated among smaller cliques that develop within the system. Among the students studied, there were seven main channels of information diffusion with considerable overlapping among them (see Figure 1): students 9, 13, and 14—13 and 14 shared an office, also often used by 9; students 9, 11, and 21 shared an apartment; students 10, 11, and 21 had offices in the same corner of the Central Building, while students 10 and 11 had a studying arrangement together, in which 21, at times, participated; students 13, 14, 15, and 16 had offices in close proximity; students 2 and 19 who reported only a fair amount of communication with each other, but who became much closer as examinations approached, studying together, sharing notetaking, and increasing their social interactions in other ways; students 17, 19, and the spouse of 17—19 visited with 17 and spouse and they talked a great deal about examinations; and students 6 and 8, both of whom were located in a smaller building, and also talked a great deal about the examinations.

Students who connected cliques played the role of gatekeepers. Information and cues obtained by the students would be passed on most often to other cliques only when the gatekeepers thought this information interesting or valuable enough to transmit. It is not our argument that this was accomplished on a level of awareness. Rather, information reached some person occupying an important link in the system. If he considered it important, he was likely to relay the information; if he perceived it as trivial, he was likely to forget it or ignore it. In the quote below a student described how information was relayed through the system.

Y [student] said that he heard from [student *X*] that [Professor *T*] told [student *X*] that the faculty has been kicking around the idea that people should only retake areas in which they fail, which to most of us would seem a very sensible way of doing it. I think this has buoyed the spirits of everyone who has heard it since I disseminated the information to a number of people since I picked it up. We all felt quite sure that since [Professor *T*] has verbalized this to [student *X*], it must be near "consumption" or something, or otherwise he would have just been quiet about it or something like that. But we really don't know if this is the case or not. But all of those to whom I have spoken of it have been very pleased by this prospect. . . . I've spoken of it with quite a number of people. . . . We mused about the prospect together.

On further investigation we found that *Y* mentioned it not only to the student making the report but to others as well. The student reporting indicated that he had passed this information on to three or four other students. In short, the extent of diffusion of information is a function of the perceived importance of the information as viewed from the perspective of persons occupying communication links. In this case, since the information was perceived as important and was both gratifying and relieving to those who heard it, it was transmitted not only along one chain but in many directions at the same time. Figure 1 only reports communication of some intensity. There were other less frequent communication links. Within the Central Building, for example, almost everyone knew everyone else. Therefore, should some information of great importance be available, it would be likely to travel circuits not pictured in the diagram although the communication links pictured were the ones most commonly used.

It was suggested earlier that all forms of adaptive behaviors traveled the communication circuits described. A student might obtain some information or think of a comforting reassurance and pass it along to those close to him in the communication structure; how far this may travel is largely dependent on the value attributed to the information by the receiver. For example, let us take an instance of a reassurance. During one of the research interviews, student 21 reported that the faculty might expect less of the second-year group than earlier groups who had taken the preliminary examinations, because the second-year group had been in the department a shorter time than previous examination-taking groups (see Figure 1). He indicated that he had discussed this idea with student 9 and was not sure whether to take it seriously or not. It appeared that this reassurance had originated with student 9, who communicated a great deal with student 21. Since a student questionnaire was being prepared at the time, the following item was included and students were asked to indicate how true they felt the item to be.

The faculty expects less from this year's student group as compared with earlier groups, because most of the people in the present group have been here for only two years.

Students were presented with four responses: "true," "partly true," "partly false," and "false." Of the twenty-two students who responded to this item, only six responded that the item was either "true" or "partly true." Everyone responding "true" or "partly true" to this item was on the main central communication chain. This chain included students 9, 10, 11, 12, 13, 14, 15, 16, 20, 21, and 23. This is not necessarily proof that this idea was discussed; mention of such discussion did come up a number of times in the student interviews, however, and it appears likely that this idea was widely communicated, especially in the Central Building. That students did not report this information "true" does not necessarily mean that they did not receive it. Certainly it is possible that this information was received and then rejected. However, the differences noted in Table 7 are suggestive of communication differences.

Table 7—Location on Central Communication Chain and Reporting Faculty Leniency for Second-Year Group

	NUMBER OF STUDENTS REPORTING ITEM	
	True or Partly True	Partly False or False
Those on central communication link	6	5
All those not on the central communication link	0	11

The foregoing raises a significant point, which will be thoroughly discussed at various places in this exposition—that modes of active coping and reassurance are usually consensual. The student will not continue to maintain perceptions and evaluations about the examinations that are clearly rejected by his peers. He will maintain these views only as long as he receives support from others. Even the seemingly ludicrous statements that students might make about the examinations usually will have some basis in social support or external cues that are consistent with the retention of the adaptive device. Should too many dissonant cues appear and should his information be openly rejected by the students he communicates with, it is likely that the student himself will reject his reassurance and find other defenses receiving more support from the environment.

Before moving on to the specific ways in which students view the preliminary examinations, let us illustrate how a belief may thrive at one point in the communication system yet seem to be less active at other points. On the questionnaire the students were asked to indicate how true the following statements were:

1. The faculty are favorably impressed by students who seem anxious about examinations.

2. It is important that the faculty think the student puts a great deal of effort into his examination preparation.

Eight students reported the first statement "true," while six indicated the latter to be "true." Four students replied that they considered both statements "true." They were students 5, 6, 7, and 8, all of whom occupied building four (see Figure 1). These four students (all defined as physical semi-isolates) shared a belief structure that received little validation from students in other buildings. How did this group develop its unique definition of the meanings of examinations?

The reasons became clear in the student interviews. Students 6, 7, and 8 had failed to pass the examinations at the Ph.D. level on previous attempts. These three students—especially 6 and 8—had formed a strong and hostile coalition against the examination system, which was essentially a way of dealing with their prior failures. They reinforced not only each other's hostilities toward the process but also each other's ideas that the examinations were subjectively evaluated and were graded on the basis of factors other than performance. One of these students felt rather strongly that his examination on a prior occasion had been evaluated not on his performance but rather on what the faculty had perceived as his attitude toward examinations, and that his failure had been due to the erroneous opinion that he had not prepared adequately. He felt this had been the major criterion for evaluating his performance; and, whether or not this was correct, sufficient realistic cues did exist to make his evaluation seem credible to others in his group, especially those who also had failed to pass on a prior attempt.

[This student] felt that one of the reasons they had not passed him was that they didn't think that he had studied much. And there was a rumor around the department that he wasn't very well prepared. I mentioned to him that, even just a few months ago, I was talking to one of the students and she also had heard this rumor; and she said, "Everyone knows [he] didn't prepare for the examinations." And when I told him this, he was really quite angry.

In one case this fellow apparently gave the impression that he wasn't studying for the examinations, and this is one reason why he feels he didn't pass. Although he thinks he did as well as many who passed, it was the impression that he shouldn't pass because he didn't put in enough effort.

Student 5, the only second-year student in this building, was more skeptical about many of the attitudes held by students 6, 7, and 8. But as he was sufficiently confused as to what had led to failure to pass at the Ph.D. level for some of the others in the past, he did accept some of the information he was exposed to, although he had some reservations as to its accuracy.

It's kind of confusing in a way. Some people liked them [the examinations] and others didn't. Some people are bitter about them—those who flunked—and some aren't. Some people are surprised they passed and some aren't. . . . [Goes on to speak of specific persons.] There are a lot of hypotheses. There is a hypothesis that he didn't know what the hell he was talking about. There was a hypothesis that he knew the stuff. He has a very hard time communicating to people. You give him a problem and he gets the right answer, but he couldn't tell you for the world how the hell he got it. . . . He can't explain what he's doing, so there is that hypothesis. Another one is that he has been here only a little over a year, and not too many people knew who he was and then they thought it was a little early to pass him. . . . Maybe they felt he hadn't been around long enough. They weren't sure whether he knew what he was doing or not. Also, there's the idea that they flunked him in order to be an incentive to other students. And then there's the idea that they flunked him because they didn't like him generally; that they did know who he was and didn't like him. . . . I don't know, there are about six ways of reasoning why he flunked. I can't for the life of me figure out which is right. . . . Now [another student], there are about three or four hypotheses why he flunked, too. And I can't say I've gotten any evidence. For a while, I've held one, and then another, and now, I've gotten to the point where I don't really know.

In short, the student taking examinations for the Ph.D. attempts to ascertain what the examinations mean, why they are given, how they are evaluated, and what the strategies are for approaching them, and then plans an approach for the anticipated examinations.

In this chapter we have attempted to indicate the relationship between physical location of students and faculty and communication in the department. We have demonstrated that physical accessibility was related to student and faculty rates of communication. The person's position in the communication structure did influence the information accessible to him, those whom he was likely to contact for social support, and how likely it was that he would receive this support. We have attempted to present data supporting the hypothesis that the communication system does play a significant role in the manner in which information and reassurances are obtained. The communication system thereby becomes essential for understanding the means through which persons meet the demands of the task and deal with the feelings evoked by the task.

Now we will look more closely at the student's perceptions of the examinations and how he goes about seeking information and planning his attack. It is in the definition of the situation that coping patterns begin to develop and mature.

4

SOURCES OF THE DEFINITION
OF THE SITUATION

Early Socialization
in the Examination Process

Graduate schools and graduate departments have their own distinctive cultures which the student must at least, in part, acquire. Particular values are maintained, specific interests are pursued, and traditions often persist, although students come and go. Each year's group has its own peculiarities, of course, and what is true of one group need not particularly be true of others. But a persistent and over-all system of assumptions and opinions may characterize a graduate department. The new graduate student learns these when he enters the department by observing older students, talking with them, and learning his way around.

The individual's exposure to the examination process comes early in his experience as a graduate student. The student's physical location, his position in the student communication structure, and his exposure to "old" students will determine what aspects of the culture he acquires and the rapidity with which he will learn them. Early in his first year the new graduate student develops some friendly relationships with second-year students. When these older students begin preparing for examinations, the first-year students very quickly sense their importance and the concern they stimulate, as the following quotes show:

It hit most of us last spring when the second-year group then was first preparing to take them. And, of course, you saw two or three people who were not quite themselves and you saw a lot of people kind of drugged up here and there, and I think this was the first time that I actually perceived what all this really meant, the magnitude of the whole thing. As an undergraduate when I applied, and I read the requirements, it didn't have much impact. I guess it wasn't until I had really been here a while that I realized that this was a pretty big step, that I would have to take it eventually. So it did bother me a little but when I saw these people last year, and I think it was not just myself but several of us who talked about the thing together. We all realized that this was something we had never been through and probably wouldn't encounter again.

Actually, I became concerned about them [the examinations] last year . . . the second term when some of my friends in the second-year class were beginning to take them. And we could sort of see what they were going through as they were doing it. We could see the gradual deterioration, the tremendous anxiety which was building up within them, the change in their external behavior. It was pretty evident. I think it was the first time that we all realized that this was something that was hanging over our heads and it was a question of time.

Nearly all of the students in the second-year group reported a similar experience. During examination period some of the first-year students would get together to discuss the implications of the examinations for them. The faculty also helped in socializing the students to the examinations by making references to them and legitimizing their importance. Some of the faculty would jokingly make references to examinations in their classroom discussions. When they might say, for example, "This would make a good question for doctoral examinations," the interest was sensed by the student as a further cue that the examinations were important indeed. In the following passage an instructor described the sensitivity of students to faculty suggestions about examinations:

If you mention the words, *written examinations,* or say, for instance, "[a particular question] is really a favorite on written examinations," they perk up like you have just given them a shot or something. They start taking notes. They are very early indoctrinated into the meaning that this has. . . . I think because it's communicated to them by the second-year students or those taking the examinations who want to impress upon them that they have been around a year; that they [the first-year students] are going to have to undergo this [same] rite.

In general, the students reported that this experience aroused their anxiety. One student explained why:

Last year when the people were taking the examinations, I witnessed the stress they appeared to be under and the changes in their behavior that seemed to be brought about. . . . When some of the people didn't make it last year, this too was pretty upsetting. Some people who I would have predicted to make it, didn't. This was essentially when I began being seriously concerned about them.

In any given group of students, anxiety over the coming situation and how early the anxiety appears will be a function of the extent to which the stress experienced by the group taking examinations is visible to the younger students. For example, first-year students who were isolated from this experience became concerned about examinations considerably later and did not become quite as concerned as those students more centrally located within the student group. The isolated student also started studying for examinations at a much later date and, on the whole, spent less time studying for them.

If this early examination socialization were not a peculiar aberration of the group under study, we would expect that we might find similar reactions among the present first-year students who observed this group taking examinations. A number of first-year students were asked, therefore, to describe their feelings during the period in which the group studied was taking the examinations. Many of the first-year students showed considerable concern over their prospects.

The great strain and stress that some candidates were undergoing during the examinations brought to me the thought of a similar experience that I may possibly have next spring when I take the examinations. I had great sympathy for some who were not even getting sleep during the examination period.

During the preparation period I felt fairly anxious about taking them next year. . . . Some of them were anxious, in general, some anxious about areas, some philosophical about the whole thing.

After the initial exposure to the examination situation, the pressing demands of other work made the examinations less salient for the student. Not until the examinations actually approached did they become a prime concern, although from time to time the student did think about them and experience some anxiety. Once the examinations neared, the student began to seek information actively and to plan his approach.

Some Comments on Adaptation

Since the picture of examinations that students develop cannot be discussed independently of adaptation, some remarks on the latter are therefore necessary. The individual's definition of the situation is dependent on the means he has to deal with it. Thus, as was pointed out earlier, the sources and magnitude of stress depend on the ability of the individual to reverse it and the efforts required of him. When we speak of an *adaptive device,* we refer to any thought or behavior that is relevant to one's situation, or to his feelings about the situation. When the behavior has consequences relevant to the situational demands, we shall refer to it as *coping behavior.* In other words, coping behaviors are relevant to defining, attacking, and meeting the task. When the behavior is aimed at handling feeling states evoked by the situation and the coping process, it will be called *defense;* thus, *defense* refers to the maintenance of the integration of personality and the control of feeling states.

These dual functions of adaptation have been noted in the work of Parsons[1] and Bales.[2] In their analyses of group processes they have recognized two components—instrumental and socioemotional behavior. Group functioning requires both. Task orientation results in the de-

1. Talcott Parsons, *The Social System* (New York: The Free Press of Glencoe, 1951).

2. Robert Bales, *Interaction Process Analysis* (Cambridge: Addison-Wesley, 1950).

velopment of various tensions that must be reduced if the group is to continue effectively its instrumental behavior. The human personality faces a similar problem. He must utilize his resources to be effective. But continued utilization of resources or coping which makes accomplishment possible also requires the reduction of tensions.

Coping and defense techniques may be more or less functional, and may receive varying amounts of recognition, support, or opposition. In sum, adaptive devices include all relevant response to the situation, functional or otherwise. The evaluation of the functional potential or capacity of any device poses a serious if not a soluble problem. Criteria for judgments of the utility of any device are not clear. One obvious difficulty is the fact that any behavior may have long-range as well as short-run significance. Indeed, what may be functional from one point of view may be questionable in the consideration of the individual's future needs. Dealing with the immediate functional significance of any act as one variable and with

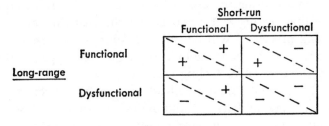

Figure 2

its effects on the person's future needs as another, varying interpretations of the functional value of any act are made possible (see Figure 2).

We can clearly agree that an act has functional significance only if it has both short-run and long-range functional consequences. Should there be some inconsistency in the short-run and long-range consequences $(+, -)$ or $(-, +)$, evaluation is extremely difficult. A student, for example, may perceive one of the suggested courses in his department as highly threatening, difficult, and reason for considerable anxiety. Thus he may avoid taking the course and for the moment reduce his feelings of discomfort, but his failure to take the course may leave him deficient in skills important for his later effectiveness. There are no criteria for establishing whether this would or would not be functional for this person. It is conceivable, for example, that should the individual not defend himself in the immediate situation, he might not survive; he might flunk out of the program or "break down." Therefore, we cannot assess the functional value of behavior merely by considering long-range consequences. On the other hand, it is similarly difficult to regard short-run effects in general, as indicative of functional value. Thus, the idea of functional adaptation serves as a sensitizing approach rather than a clearly defined and refined set of ideas that may be operationalized effectively.

Student Perception of the Examinations and Adaptation

We shall now attempt to show how the point of view developed by the student regarding examinations may be seen as an adaptive process. Listed in Table 8 are student and faculty responses to questions concerning nine possible functions of examinations. In each case they were asked to indicate the applicability of the listed function to the present examination situation.[3]

3. The reader will notice that data are presented for twenty-two faculty members in Table 8 as compared with only twenty faculty members in

In general, there seemed to be considerable similarity in the extent to which various faculty and students attributed applicability to the various functions of examinations. Students, somewhat more than faculty, seemed to emphasize the nonobjective aspects of examinations. For example, while students emphasized the elimination of undesirable personalities as a function of examinations, the faculty more often emphasized the examinations as an

Table 8—Student and Faculty Reports of the Applicability of Various Functions to the Examination Situation

| | PER CENT OF | | |
| | 22 Students Reporting Very or | 22 Faculty Reporting Very or | |
Functions	Fairly Applicable	Fairly Applicable	Difference
An objective evaluation of student ability	67	73	+ 6
An objective evaluation of student knowledge	77	86	+ 9
An attempt to make the student organize his thinking	73	82	+ 9
An attempt to get the student to study intensively	82	95	+13
A method of weeding out incompetents	59	77	+18
A method of weeding out undesirable personalities	36	9	—27
An initiation rite	41	41	0
An attempt to depersonalize the evaluation of students	55	73	+18
A test of the students' ability to handle stress	59	45	—14

earlier tables. These two additional faculty members were an acting instructor who had just completed his Ph.D. in the department and a new assistant professor who had no formal teaching functions. Neither was listed as department faculty and the researcher did not become aware of them for some time. Both were asked, however, to complete a questionnaire and were included as part of the faculty in analysis of questionnaire responses.

instrument to eliminate incompetents and as an attempt to depersonalize the evaluation of students.

Included on the questionnaire were a number of other items relevant to how students and faculty view the examinations. Both were asked to indicate the truth or falsity of the following items: most students who failed preliminary examinations in the past have had difficult personalities; the examinations are like a game—if the student plays it by the rules, he is bound to pass; if faculty members like the student, he has a better chance of having a favorable outcome on the examinations; and the decision as to who will pass and who will fail is made prior to examinations. If indeed the students more than the faculty believed that the examinations were nonobjective, they should have attested more readily than faculty to the truth of the preceding statements. In regard to the first two items, students were more likely to assert these were true than did faculty. However, the differences were not very large. While 29 per cent of the students reported as "true" or "partly true" a statement of association between failure and being a difficult personality, only 14 per cent of the faculty made such a report. Also, while 45 per cent of the students saw some truth in the notion that the examinations were a game, only 32 per cent of the faculty made a similar report. In regard to the third item student and faculty opinion are shown in Table 9.[4] As analysis of that table discloses, students were more likely than faculty to indicate this item as "true" or "partly true." Table 10 shows student and faculty opinion about the fourth item.

Since all the results are in the same direction, with

4. Responses are indicated for only twenty-one faculty members as one member failed to respond to the question. Subsequent deviations from twenty-two responses for both students and faculty are due to the failure of one or another person to respond to that particular item.

Table 9—Student and Faculty Evaluations of the Truth of the Item, "If Faculty Members Like the Student, He Has a Better Chance of Having a Favorable Outcome on the Examinations"

| | PER CENT | |
Response	Students (N-22)	Faculty (N-21)
"True" or "Probably True"	82	43
"Probably False," or "False"	18	57

Table 10—Student and Faculty Evaluations of the Truth of the Item, "The Decision as to Who Will Pass and Who Will Fail Is Made Prior to the Examinations"

| | PER CENT | |
Response	Students (N-22)	Faculty (N-21)
Some truth	68	5
No truth at all	32	95

considerable association between student status and the indication that the decision about who will pass and who will fail is made prior to the examinations, there was substantial support for our assertion that students do emphasize the nonobjective aspects of the examinations while faculty emphasize the more objective attributes. Students also were somewhat more likely than faculty to assert that the likeability of the student is a factor in evaluating him, that decisions about who will pass and who will fail are to some extent made beforehand, and that the student who can maintain good relationships with faculty is in a better position relative to examinations than one who fails to do this.

The discrepancies between student and faculty evaluations of the examination process are indicative of the adaptive devices students use. In the interviews students frequently would discuss the examinations, emphasizing their nonobjective aspects without denying their objectivity. Their ambiguous view of examinations allowed them to see them much as their needs demanded at any moment. The student descriptions of the examinations seemed to have the function of placing responsibility for possible failure outside the student. By viewing the examinations as, in some measure, subjective, the student thus was able to control the situation's possible effect on his self-image. Should he fail, he could attribute his failure to the whimsical, inaccurate, and subjective evaluations of the faculty. Thus an attempt was made to insulate the self from impending attack.

Adaptation takes much more subtle and complex forms than the data presented might suggest. Between reassuring cognitions and the reality limits of the situation, the student treads a thin line. Rationalizations that are too obvious are not effective, for they cannot be readily upheld in the light of contradictory and nonconfirmatory evidence that the student must constantly encounter. For this reason, social support becomes important, as is the student's attempt to qualify his attitudes sufficiently so that they appear realistic and also do not interfere with adequate preparation for the examinations. Thus, the very same student who will indicate that the examinations do take into account personality, likeability, and playing the game also can see the examinations as an objective evaluation of knowledge and ability, and as an attempt to make the student study intensively and organize his thinking.

Student attitudes are more understandable when one examines the content of the statements they make in relation to their student status. The expressions of students vary considerably: some, thinking that they have made a poor impression in the past, find a need to see the examinations as objective; others prefer to see the process as a subjective one, depending on where they see themselves relative to other students in past performance and on their level of preparation to meet the situation.

The students who view the examinations as least objective are those who have failed the examinations on prior attempts. In a way, their statements are a reaction to failing to pass the examinations. By seeing the examinations as nonobjective, the student can shift responsibility from the self to external factors. Also, as we will show later, those who had failed previously have the greatest anxiety. Perception of the examinations as a function of bias allows the student to insulate the self against a second failure which, if seen by the student as a product of his own incompetence, would be extremely painful. In the following passage a student who had failed described his perceptions of examinations when he took them for the first time, and then his thoughts on his second attempt:

First Time: The first time I went into the examinations with a very idealistic picture of the examinations and the department. I felt like it should be a fairly valid procedure. . . . Of course, I hadn't given much thought to it. . . . I went into the examination with the attitude that if I had learned anything, it would measure it. The question about the validity of the examinations came when I discovered that I failed the areas in which I had a tremendous amount of study. . . .

Second Time: Some persons have a major advisor to represent their case, but unfortunately, our past failure was because we didn't have any major advisor to represent our case and it seems unfortunate that that is the way people are evaluated. Presumably, we're supposed to be evaluated in terms of our performance on the examination but this is not true, apparently, as I see it. . . . Evaluation is just a subjective evaluation from the faculty members attending the final meeting to decide on whether a person will pass or fail . . . and I think that . . . their personal evaluations of the student is probably the crucial thing.

It is essential to recognize that the student who builds a cognitive defense system does so by utilizing actual situations and cues that are credible. For example, there are faculty decision meetings, and it is recognized that at times extra-examination performance criteria are discussed in reference to students. The faculty meeting, which is private and rarely discussed by faculty members, serves as an excellent point to anchor a plausible defensive-cognitive plan. This is usually not accomplished on a level of awareness—the attitudes and evaluations that the students express are usually perceived as accurate perceptions subject, of course, to error.

The attitude we have already described is typical of those who have failed in the past, especially those who had expected to pass on their prior attempt. Although students may exaggerate the subjective elements in the examination process, examinations to some extent probably are subjective, and it is the signs of subjectivism that the student recognizes and utilizes in structuring his comforting cognitive frame of reference.

As yet, it is not too clear why the student should find nonobjectivity comforting. One might suspect the opposite. For, if the student had been failed before for being a difficult personality, why not again? Here the student makes an interesting cognitive shift. He now argues that, while the faculty originally made its judgment of him on the basis of insufficient and inaccurate information, they have in the interim period acquired more reliable information and have changed their subjective evaluation so that they now are inclined to see him pass. This attitude, expressed in various ways, is not often as obviously stated as we have implied. It is usually modified and associated with various cues the student has recognized so that it appears plausible.

In a later chapter, the reactions of students to failure will be discussed in greater detail. At this point, it will suffice to recognize that of the students who held most tenaciously to the opinion that subjective evaluation is as important a factor as performance, those who had failed previously served as opinion-makers. The reason for this reaction to failure is obvious to those who have gone through the experience. A student who had passed made the following observation about those who had failed:

This is such a wound. People who fail it just get almost paralyzed . . . except the few who have someone really give them a push. A couple will not take it again. One waited a year and a half. He underwent a terrible personality change. He began getting more paranoid, more reclusive, and much more idiosyncratic than before. And other people who have failed it who I have observed have been crushed by it. They were quite demoralized after examinations, and have been paralyzed in terms of really buckling down. . . . To go through another three months of this compulsive studying day after day after day is just insane. . . . Their whole concept of themselves just dropped terribly. They feel sort of empty, worthless.

The second-year student, although he holds similar attitudes about the lack of examination objectivity, will maintain them with less tenacity and express more uncertainty about the validity of his opinions. In part, his views are influenced by the reported experiences of the older students who have failed in the past, as well as by those who have passed, and it becomes necessary for him to piece together some picture of examinations from the conflicting and contradictory fragments which he encounters. Also, the physical location of the second-year student and, hence, his exposure to rumors affect his views.

Accessibility and centrality in the student group influenced the number of stories that students were likely to have heard about others' past experiences with the examinations and provided opportunity for discussion of the possible functions and meanings the examinations might have. The centrally located students, who considered more functions of the examinations, were less certain about what the functions were than the more isolated students. Note the following statements made by centrally located students:

The biggest issue was what they were supposed to measure; whether they were measuring intelligence—whether this was a three-day new type of intelligence test. If so, why wait until we've been here two years to give us this? If it is a measure of academic achievement, why won't the course grades be sufficient? If it's a weeding-out process to get rid of undesirable people, then these sorts of people shouldn't have been let in in the first place. . . . We were trying to assess the rationale of the examinations and especially the rationale for why the people who passed, passed, and the people who failed, failed, in the past.

You are going into a situation where you have virtually no control over it whatsoever, and yet, perhaps your entire future may be dependent on how well you do. By that very fact it cannot help but be a very stressful situation. . . . There is the feeling that these examinations provide a very good opportunity to get rid of students they feel are pretty poor, not only in terms of what they know, but also in terms of personality characteristics. If they don't truly feel that this person has what it takes to be successful in the field personality-wise, it's a great time really to get rid of him. There's sort of a feeling that this has been done in the past. It's part of the rumor that floats around. . . . This is a body of rumor that has sprung up in terms of "I have done fairly well in the past few years. Although I may not do well on the examinations, they will take this into account." They are . . . not aiming to throw you out of school and so forth . . . I can't really verify any of it.

However, the views offered by isolated students and those less central in the communication structure were quite different. These students, having a great deal less to say about examinations, were likely to mention fewer subjective criteria in discussing the functions of examinations. Even when they had heard some of these subjective evaluations, they tended to give them less attention.

It's sort of a weeding out of the able from the unable in a way. . . . I don't really think they are the finest instrument there is, but I can't really think of a better one.

They need something to see how much you have picked up in graduate school.

To test a person's degree of knowledge and skill. . . . The primary importance is weeding out people who are not qualified.

It isn't really objective but it is as objective as it can be. . . . An adequate student can give an adequate answer. . . . I'm less informed as to different individuals' biases and I really don't know very many members of the department because I don't stay around [Central Building] very often.

Perception of Factors
Differentiating Passers from Failers

Both students and faculty were asked, "What three factors would you say are most important in differentiating those students who have passed and those who have failed in past examinations?" The result in general followed the pattern described earlier in the chapter. Whereas both faculty and students recognized knowledge, preparation, and organization as the prime factors in determining outcomes on examinations, students consistently gave more weight to nonacademic factors than did faculty members. Student and faculty reaction to two of these factors—ability to throw the bull and being well organized—were especially striking. In regard to the former, 23 per cent of the students reported this a factor, while no faculty member checked this item. On the other hand, while 73 per cent of the faculty members considered the second item an important factor, only 41 per cent of the students acknowledged it as such. Both results were indicative of the student tendency to emphasize the nonobjective aspects of examinations more than would the faculty, while faculty, more than the student, emphasized the objective aspects (see Table 11).

Table 11—Student and Faculty Reports of Factors Differentiating Students Who Have Passed and Students Who Have Failed Examinations

Factors	PERCENTAGE OF PERSONS IN EACH GROUP INDICATING THE FACTOR AS ONE OF THE THREE MOST IMPORTANT FACTORS DIFFERENTIATING PASSERS FROM FAILERS	
	Students (N-22)	Faculty (N-22)
Ability to deal with anxiety	32	36
Knowledge	73	86
Intelligence	14	27
Good personality (well-liked)	14	0
Amount of preparation	55	41
Ability to create the impression of being hardworking	27	14
Ability to throw the bull	23	0
Demonstration of research competence	23	18
Being well organized	41	73
Others	—	9

The students often seek information as to why other students in the past have had the outcomes they had. To the extent that they find the outcomes reasonable and consistent with their perceptions of the student, and that they themselves do not have similar shortcomings, they can derive considerable comfort from such analysis. Witness the following appraisals made by students:

Every one of the people that flunked, there's some personality factor that I could maybe say was the cause of it. . . . Of the people who did well, not only did I feel that they were competent in talking with them and that they were studying . . . but they were also the kinds of people that get along generally. . . . They probably are above average generally in their ability to talk to people, and have all the social skills maybe. On the other hand, the people who flunked I would say are just the opposite.

I guess post-hoc judgments have been made on almost everyone who failed them. With the ones I've been familiar with, there has always been something which again from a post-hoc view . . . has appeared quite obvious. . . . Looking at them after the fact, it seemed almost obvious that the person had a good chance of failing. One sign would be working very slowly, or making no progress toward the completion of the Master's thesis, or doing academic or decent research. Another sign would be under-achieving in coursework, passing but at a minimum level. Another sign would be the alienation of certain faculty members . . . key faculty members. . . . Another would be being here too long and putting off the writtens until say your fifth year, as happened last year. One boy finally got around to taking them in the fifth year and he was failed. The feeling seemed to be that the faculty was patting him on the behind, scolding him for waiting so long.

The examples were many, but what is most important is that the student had a tendency to attribute more import to nonobjective factors in the evaluation of the examinations than did faculty members. The development of the student's concept of what the examinations encompass, the information he acquires, and the extent of his descriptions were associated with his social position and experience in the department. In the coming section this experience will be analyzed more thoroughly so that the threat components of the students' situation can be better understood.

Sources of Stress

In Chapter 1 some definitions of stress were discussed and the preliminary Ph.D. examinations were pointed to as the primary threat situation under study. Both the meanings that students attributed to the situation and the extent to which the students' self-respect, future plans, and associations with others were dependent on their success in the examinations were examined. It was noted also how the student's status in the department, his past experience with doctoral examinations, and familial obligations increased what he perceived to be the threatening aspects of the situation.

How are we to evaluate the degree of stress experienced by the students? Within the group studied anxiety was most frequently reported verbally, although fear of failure and depression often were evident and discussed. Among psychiatrists there is considerable debate as to whether fear, anxiety, and depression are correlated with different biochemical and endocrinological states; most would agree, however, that fear, anxiety, and depression are stress responses. Grinker and Spiegel, for example, write: "The . . . differences between fear and anxiety are less important than their similarities, since the feeling-tone and the physiological concomitants in anxiety and fear are identical. Furthermore, there are no pure fears inasmuch as all external dangers also have symbolic sig-

nificance."[5] The decision was made, therefore, to attempt
to measure stress by taking into account all recognizable,
discomforting responses (anxiety, depression, fear, and so
on). Since anxiety was reported most commonly, we shall
frequently refer to it as our measure of stress. Data for
rating students on the degree of stress experienced were
available from three sources: student self-ratings of anxiety, students' ratings of each other's levels of anxiety, and
the researcher's observations of students during interviews
concerning examinations. These data had various deficiencies. The student self-ratings of anxiety were not
very valuable, since most students reported themselves
fairly anxious or about as anxious as other students. Only
three students reported themselves very anxious, and four
as not very anxious. The student ratings of the anxiety
of other students were best when the student rated was
centrally located and, therefore, visible to the group. In
cases where the student in question was physically isolated, other students either refused to rate his anxiety or
made a guess. The investigator, therefore, attributed
greatest weight to his own ratings of the degree of anxiety
students manifested, since he had ample opportunity to
observe the students carefully over a period of several
months. Using as part of his rating both student self-ratings and student ratings of each other, the final ratings
were made prior to the analysis and the researcher made
every effort to assess stress independently of other data.

Three categories of stress were used: high, moderate,
and low. The student ratings of one another were used
only in the cases where students showed some assurance in
their ratings. Thus, ratings for thirteen students were
available. In ten of these thirteen cases there was agree-

5. R. R. Grinker and J. P. Spiegel, *Men Under Stress* (New York:
McGraw-Hill Book Co., Inc., 1945), p. 120.

ment with the researcher's ratings. In the other three cases there was a discrepancy of one stress category. In these cases the investigator's ratings were used as they had been in the other ten cases where student ratings were not based on frequent interpersonal contact.

The ratings of stress used in this study were short of the scientific ideal of reliable quantitative ratings. It should be recalled, however, that we were dealing with stress over time, and that this is more difficult to measure than stress at a given point in time, which in itself is a difficult problem. Although the ratings are not as formal as we would like, they do, I think, approximate the experiences of the students under study.

Let us now view the relationship of student status, patterns of student communication about examinations, and stress.

Table 12—Student Status, Extent of Communication, and Level of Stress

| Student Status | Number of Students STRESS | | | |
	High	Moderate	Low	Total
Older Students				
With 3 or more communication links	2	0	0	2
With less than 3 communication links	4	2	1	7
Second Year Students				
With 3 or more communication links	2	3	1	6
With less than 3 communication links	0	2	6	8
Total	8	7	8	23

As examination of Table 12 shows, the low-stress persons were primarily second-year students who had less than three communication links. Six of the eight low-stress persons were in this category. It is also clear that older students were more anxious about examinations than were the younger. While six of the nine older students were high-stress individuals, only two of the fourteen second-year students were rated as high-stress. Also, students who communicated more about examinations were more anxious than lesser communicators. Of the eight students with three or more communication links, seven were either high- or moderate-stress persons. Of the fifteen students with less than three communication links, only eight were high- or moderate-stress persons. It might be suspected that students who became concerned about examinations were likely to seek to relieve their stress by finding support, reassurances, and the like from others in the group. Although this no doubt did occur, considerable interaction concerning examinations also became cause for anxiety, as we will show in the following section.

Interaction and Other Circumstances Likely to Elicit Stress Response

Although we have chosen the preliminary examinations as the primary threatening situation to which students had to adapt, it is important to recognize that, while they were an important source of stress, discomfort often was evoked by other stimuli related to the examinations. The duration of the pre-examination preparation period, the high motivation of students, and the importance of the examinations—all created the conditions for a number of other stimuli associated with the examinations to elicit stress responses.

Although, theoretically, it was possible for the entire group to pass, most of the students felt that some probably would fail. This created a highly competitive situation within the department. Thirteen of the twenty-two students reported that they felt they were competing with other students in their group. Of these thirteen, seven had three or more communication links of fair or great intensity with other students about examinations. Of the nine students who reported that they were not competing with others, only one of these had three or more communication links about examinations. Thus communication and competition within the department were associated. Most indicative of the intense departmental competition was the way in which students compared themselves with one another.

Social Comparison as a Source of Stress

The competitiveness of the system under study has already been noted. Although it was theoretically possible that all students taking examinations could pass, students primarily evaluated themselves and their chances by comparing their abilities and performances with those of their peers, and their feelings of adequacy were largely dependent on how they saw themselves relative to their associates. As Festinger[6] has noted, social comparison is more prevalent in situations where criteria for evaluating oneself are, at best, rather obscure. In situations where an outside objective standard is not available, as in the cases of the students under study, some standard for self-judgment must be established. Since, to a large extent, the subject matter of their discipline is interpretive and since no student can completely master even a small section of the literature in his areas, students will judge their worth relative to their peers, and evaluate their knowledge and competence relative to the other students taking examina-

---

6. Leon Festinger, "A Theory of Social Comparison Processes," in P. Hare, E. Borgatta, and R. Bales, *Small Groups* (New York: Alfred A. Knopf, 1955), pp. 163-187.

tions. And, when such a comparison leads to unfavorable indications or judgments, it may be a source of considerable anxiety—as when a student, for example, discovers that the other students seem better prepared to take the examinations than he is.

The importance of the structure of the examination process in inducing stress cannot be overemphasized. Students were asked to do an impossible job: to prepare adequately in nine different areas and, at the same time, to attend to their usual course and assistantship duties. Since fully adequate preparation was virtually impossible, the student could gauge his progress and chances only in terms of what other students seemed to be doing. The difficulty of preparing adequately emphasized, of course, one's competitive performance. The student recognized that the academic system functions to turn out students; should the entire group fail, no matter how poorly they performed, the adequacy of the faculty and its operation would be in question rather than the performance of the student group. Thus, realistically, irrespective of the verbalized values, students do compete and also are graded competitively. This of course accentuated the social comparison process.

After the early interviews students were given ten items that they had mentioned from time to time on a questionnaire and were asked to indicate both how often they had the experience mentioned in each item and how likely that experience was to arouse their anxiety.

Of all the students in Table 13, who compared themselves with others to some extent, 73 per cent reported that this made them anxious. Another indication of social comparison (having someone else mention something one is unfamiliar with) aroused anxiety in 82 per cent of the cases. Only one item elicited a report of higher anxi-

Table 13—Student Reports of Anxiety Experiences

	PER CENT	
Anxiety Items	Students Who Reported Having Experience	All Students Who Indicated that This Experience Made Them Very or Fairly Anxious
Talking about examinations with persons who are very anxious	100	59
Talking about examinations with persons who are less anxious than you are	100	41
Comparing yourself to other students	100	73
Not understanding something in class that other students seem to understand	95	64
Having someone mention a name, book, or a study that is important and that you are unfamiliar with	100	82
Being unable to concentrate and study as much as you like	100	91
Wasting time	100	77
Thoughts of panicking	73	45
Not understanding a book you are reading	100	55
Finding yourself unable to sleep	59	41

ety, that dealing with the inability to concentrate and study. But this item also is important from the point of view of social comparison, for the student knows that other students are studying and that his inability to concentrate thus puts him in an unfavorable competitive position.

Students' Awareness of "Threat"

The student began to get some idea of the dimensions and sources of anxiety as he observed other groups taking the examinations. Before he actually experiences the situation, he is likely already to have learned something from other students about methods of avoiding and dealing with anxiety. He learns from others' mistakes and attempts to capitalize on their experiences. One of the older students, in the passage that follows, describes how his group learned by trial and error that study group sections stimulated considerable anxiety. Younger students, observing the stimulation of anxiety, avoided such sessions without first attempting them.

Candidate: As I remember, we had sessions about a week or two weeks before. We would get together in the evenings and we would take a particular area and ask each other questions, and try and contribute material that was sort of our own to the rest of the group. It was sort of a cooperative venture. . . . And for a while these weren't too anxiety-provoking but then, when it got down toward the end, people started bringing up things that you just didn't know, and we'd get quite anxious. We had to discontinue it. For a time, there was a great deal of anxiety around the department.

Second-year Student: People in our group seem to avoid talking about it more than other people. Last spring, for example, the group that was taking it had study meetings and this sort of thing, where they would all get together. And this year, these things are being religiously avoided . . . I think because we observed that people came out and I don't think they disseminated too much information. They were tremendously anxiety-provoking. And I think it's avoidance of anxiety that's doing this. People this year are very much on their own.

Anxiety seemed to be most effectively stimulated by two types of individuals—the competent student and the student who is himself very anxious. In the former case, students inevitably compared themselves unfavorably in a competitive sense with this person and this proved anxiety-provoking; in the latter case, the student generated and communicated anxiety.

The student who is highly competent and competitive can make others feel exceptionally vulnerable. Not only did the best students often stimulate each other's anxiety, they sometimes aroused one another to even a greater extent than they did students of lesser ability. It may be that whereas the average student did not see himself as competing with the few top students, the top students competed among themselves, as the following statement indicates:

I find myself thinking in competitive terms with some of the people whom I consider to be top people, which I wish I wouldn't do. . . . I find myself getting a little bit upset, say, when you're in class or when you are somewhere else and one of these people mentions something that I haven't read, or something I just haven't heard about. . . . You see, this makes me very anxious.

All of the students from time to time aroused anxiety in others by stimulating unfavorable social comparisons.

I'll talk to someone like [student X], and he'll quote a whole string of studies I've never heard of . . . and that will set me off.

When I talk to people my anxiety increases somewhat because I find that they are in better shape than I am. You just talk to them and it makes you anxious.

One student in the group—the student with the highest communication rate—was an "anxiety carrier." Below, some students report their experiences in interacting with him.

He has a very contagious kind of anxiety. . . . He's looking for support or something. . . . I really don't give too much support to him because it almost involves me taking his anxiety and catching it and him getting rid of it.

He began to talk about lowering his level of aspiration. He seemed to think his chances were so small. I began to think that mine weren't too good either.

It's funny, I've tried to stay away from [student X] this week. . . . I haven't gone out of my way to talk about examinations with him because I guess there was one day last week, he got in with [another student] and I and started to rave and rant about how much he didn't know, and I guess we got a little worried. He seems to transmit this anxiety so easily.

Situations that provide the students with the opportunity to make social comparisons that undermine their preparation and competence (their means of coping) are sources of considerable anxiety. For example, the following statements describe a situation that led to considerable anxiety for one of the students under study. Both he and another student described the situation.

Student A: [Student C] said he read 300 pages in [book X] yesterday. This is rather frightening to me since I only read about 150 in [book Y] and at the time it sort of made me feel that I was goofing off. . . . He didn't start until two in the afternoon. . . . He couldn't have read 300 pages well in that period of time. The more I thought of it, that's how I coped with my brief feelings of anxiety. He surely couldn't have gotten much out of [book X] because I read the book a couple of years ago and I really remember; it's crammed full of research.

Student B: [Student A] has been very industrious, and has read several books and has gone through the last five years of [journals], and so on, and really has covered a substantial amount of material. He kind of gets threatened if anyone approaches him in the amount that he does. . . . Late Sunday night [student C] came back to the house and told [student A] that he had read 300 pages in [book X], which seemed to be kind of strange in view of the fact that he got up very late and hadn't spent much time at the building; and while he was at the building I saw him going around and talking to people and so on. It didn't really seem as if he was putting in so much effort. Yet, he came back and claimed this, and it apparently got [student A] upset. . . . I don't know if he really didn't believe it, or that it shook him up that [student C] was doing more than he was or what. . . . [Student A] was kind of amazed at first, and also he seemed to think that it was a hostile thing. The reason [student C] was telling him this with such great elation was to make him anxious rather than to tell him about his own accomplishment.

From occasion to occasion, these three students who spent a great deal of time together stimulated each other's discomfort. As the examinations approached, there was one point at which an agreement was made among them—namely, to avoid any discussion of examinations. But the saliency of examinations in the students' orientation made this impossible. In the following statement another incident is related where one of these students made the other feel anxious.

The other night when I went home [student B] was in bed reading [book G] and I mentioned something about [some specific concepts]. He asked me about this and I told him what chapter it was in and who did the original study on it. This sort of got him real anxious because I knew this and hadn't been reading [book G] and he just that night had read it but didn't remember it.

As the reader might notice, the student who finds himself able to arouse anxiety in others will feel some gratification. This stems from the feeling not only that the student knows material other students have little grasp of, but also that other students are anxious and worried about examinations. Thus he is in a good position in the competitive situation. An individual can arouse anxiety in others if he makes the other student question either his capacity or ability to perform. As the vast and unorganized literature in the field makes it likely that all students will know some things that others do not, this is not difficult.

From a personal point of view, anxiety is an indication of threat to the "self," and, since examinations are important to the student, anxiety can be aroused by indications that he is not coping adequately with the task, the competitive situation, or both. The reference to a book, article, or study the student knows little about, the observation that others have a seemingly better approach to examinations, and stimuli that interfere with studying—all make the individual question the effectiveness of his coping.

Anxiety, however, is not always a burden. Indeed, it may play a motivating role in the student's preparation, and encourage him to put more effort and time into his studies.

Sources of Stress and Change in Mood

Students taking preliminary examinations experienced substantial fluctuations in mood. While such mood changes occur frequently among students in general, their greater frequency during the pre-examination months allowed observation of the course they took and the stimuli and perceptions with which they were associated. Although these fluctuations in mood state are seemingly "neurotic-like," they also were closely linked with certain types of stimulation from the environment, and especially with interpersonal relationships which resulted in the student making unfavorable social comparisons. On other occasions these moods were stimulated by a situation in which the student's self-confidence was undermined, and at the moment when his efforts (his ability to manipulate adaptive means) seemed to him to have all the signs of futility.

When our subjects reported mood changes, these

changes appeared to be linked to some of the anxiety stimuli we have already mentioned. Exposure to some evidence of past failure or signs of impending failure was likely to start the cycle of self-doubt, self-degradation, and intense anxiety and depression. These fluctuations sometimes were associated with going through old examinations and seeing questions that the student felt himself unable to answer. Although students who perceived themselves able to answer these questions experienced favorable mood changes, feelings of mastery were not very frequent.

Feelings of depression occurred most frequently in persons who had strong feelings of past failure, and reminders of these circumstances combined with unfavorable situational and comparison stimuli seemed to bring about strong feelings of loss of competence, confidence, and ability for mastery. One such report is indicated below:

I was teaching [course X] last semester and then was put on [course Y], which is definitely, it seems to me, a lower type job. So I get ideas that maybe they don't think much of me in the department and that's why they put me back into [course Y]. . . . One of the reasons I get depressed is because I'm working on [course Y]. . . . I just start thinking how stupid and dumb and what a slob I am. This goes on and builds up.

This report is not necessarily indicative of a personal idiosyncrasy. Both individuals who were in the position of moving from course X to course Y found working on course Y a depression stimulus and an occasion for loss of confidence in themselves and their ability. Moreover, this demotion did not go unnoticed by other students as indicative of faculty disesteem. Teaching course Y also contributed in other ways to student depression and anxi-

ety. Requiring a great deal of time and performance of
routine duties not very relevant to the written examinations, it thus served also as an annoyance and a barrier
to effective studying and, therefore, to adequate coping
attempts. A similar pattern was observed in students who
had other kinds of assistantship duties. When the student
was obliged to perform these duties, and when these duties interfered with studying, he tended to experience a
fluctuation in mood state, plus a general annoyance and
at times a disgust for the work. Accompanying these
changes in mood states were feelings of the inevitability
of failure, doubt about professional goals, and unhappy
ruminating about one's place in the scheme of things.

Mood fluctuations seemed to be associated with becoming overwhelmed by the subject matter: being overcome with the feeling that "I can never master this
material; I will never be adequately prepared." This feeling may be brought about by recognition of deficiency:
the student may read a book he cannot understand, or
be unable to follow the discussion in class or to remember
the material he is reading, or find it difficult to concentrate, and so on. These feelings of inability to master the
situation and manipulate what are perceived as the effective means became particularly great when there was some
evidence that other students were more successful in mastery. This will become clear if we analyze a specific situation and carefully observe how a mood change is brought
about.

The Pre-"Writtens" Blast

Approximately two weeks before written examinations, one of the students had an open-house party. Some
of the students attended this party with the hope that it

would provide a break from arduous studying and relief from the tension of examinations. Yet, as the saliency of examinations was high, the party turned into a grand bull session about examinations. This is particularly interesting, since most of the students reported at the time that they would have preferred to avoid any discussion of the examinations.

Such full-scale discussions about written examinations occur more and more frequently as the "writtens" approach. Agreements are made not to discuss them, and some students avoid others for this same purpose, but inevitably discussions occur. In the following statement a student describes how such discussions evolve:

There is quite a bit of interaction. And you go into a person's office and there will be one or two other people there. People will just be around. Of course, you start talking about almost anything. Invariably, the topic comes to writtens. It's almost unavoidable. It's almost like sex. So it just sort of starts.

At the party no one wanted to discuss writtens, but nevertheless the party soon did evolve into such a discussion.

I thought it would be a nice party. Everyone would just forget writtens for a while. It wasn't like that. The subject came up. I don't know, it really makes me feel anxious and depressed. I just wanted to sit in a corner. . . . I avoided it as much as I could, but you can't escape it very well. I just tried not to talk about writtens but it still bothered me. . . . I think it's really stupid to talk about it at a party.

We expected it to be a nice party, where people would be playing bridge or dancing. But to my dismay, as we walked in, there was one group of people over here, the people who were talking about the writtens, who were involved in a big general bull session about the writtens. . . . And the other group was their wives plus [student *T*] and [spouse]. And so we went directly to this group of people who were socializing and stayed there all night long. It was really pretty annoying to me. . . . I was looking for a party to be a time away from this and turn my thoughts to general social kinds of activities or just anything . . . I don't get a great deal out of these things. I find them to be anxiety arousing.

Interestingly, the bull session included primarily those students who were least anxious about examinations and who were perceived also by most of the other students to be those most competent. The two students who avoided the discussion were both rated as high-stress persons. Of the students who participated in the bull session, two were rated as moderate-stress persons, and the other two as low-stress persons. The fifth student who participated in the bull session had already passed the examinations on a previous occasion. The more anxious students avoided the discussion but at the same time felt considerable resentment that the discussion was taking place and that they were missing something. On the other hand, even those students who participated in the discussion did not find themselves immune to the arousal of anxiety. The fifth member of the group, the husband of one of the students, was giving advice to the group about how to prepare for the examinations. As a result of the session, one of the low-stress members, who was considered very able by the other students, experienced a considerable loss of confidence in himself.

[*B*] was telling us how to go about preparing for examinations. And he is a walking encyclopedia . . . as far as articles and current issues are concerned. . . . He just knows everything that has been done. And he was telling us about how to go about preparing in different areas; get an issue in each area and grind it home and things of this sort. . . . He was counseling us and, also, exhibiting his knowledge. That got me a little shook up because he does know a hell of a lot. I certainly wouldn't go into the examination with anything like that degree of competency, or at least information, and this got me a little anxious. . . . [I feel] considerably less secure since the Saturday night exchange. I don't feel as competent about my potentialities on this particular area. . . . I haven't attempted to prepare for this material and there must certainly be other areas that I'm better prepared for than these people. But it seems that [student D] and [student E] are up on this area. . . . They were bandying back all the studies and everything, and I just sort of felt lost at the time.

This student attempted to leave the situation to free himself from the anxiety stimulus:

I went over to the other people to forget about that. I really didn't forget about it. I moved away from the sphere of influence there, and then returned later when they happened to be off that kick and were just talking.

The student under discussion, although not considerably anxious about examinations as compared with many of the other students, was aroused by this incident. Such arousal also occurred with other persons classified as low stress. Every now and then they would encounter a situation that stimulated a considerable feeling of anxiety. Before this incident this particular student had been extremely effective in insulating himself against anxiety, partly because of his competence and partly because of his effective avoidance of situations that he expected would arouse anxiety. In a sense this situation caught him unawares and unprotected. It did not take long for his feelings of self-confidence to suffer.

The party incident illustrates some important points. First, it suggests that no student is really immune to anxiety stimulation. All of the students at some time reported experiencing a similar kind of anxiety attack. Some, of course, experienced these attacks more often than others. What is particularly interesting is how easily the students' self-image could be threatened, at least momentarily. This student experienced doubt not only about the areas being discussed but also about his performance in general. This was especially surprising for the student we have discussed, since most students and faculty had agreed that he was likely to be very successful in the field, and on all previous occasions he had done extremely well on all his work in the department. This experience of encountering some- one who displayed his knowledge occurred frequently to most students, and various modes of avoiding these situa- tions were developed.

To reformulate, theoretically, what we have been say- ing in this chapter: in a situation where the requirements of an adequate response are vague, or at best uncertain, individuals are likely to view their progress in terms of the progress of those around them (their peers). The attitudes they develop concerning what constitutes suc- cessful adaptation are dependent on how they perceive their adaptive potentialities as compared with others in similar situations. Since social comparison is essential in evaluating one's progress, the individual's preparation is influenced by what he perceives others to be doing and by the progress they are making. Since he is attuned to these others, indications that they have mastered material he himself has not mastered, that they are making more satis- factory progress than he, that they are retaining more than he, and the like often will induce considerable anxi- ety. In turn, anxiety states can lead to considerable self- questioning and mood changes. Students who are more isolated from the communication network and who there- fore take less part in the processes of social comparison are less informed about the examinations, feel less competitive and less anxious, and in general are less likely to experience intensive mood fluctuations.

Yet, anxiety is aroused by means other than social comparison. It is also brought about when the individual is unable to mobilize his coping and defense potentialities. Thus, students who find themselves unable to study, or those who waste time, become upset. It is essential for the individual to retain control over the situation and the task. In this instance his most effective control lies in successful studying. Should he lack this ability, he will be likely to feel threatened, as is indicated by the fact that over 90 per cent of the students reported that they became anxious when they found themselves unable to study and concentrate as effectively as they would like.

In this chapter we have not tried to discuss the subtle aspects of change in mood fluctuation or to cover all the sources of stress in the situation. We have presented, rather, a series of illustrations that show how anxiety may be aroused and generated. Of course, anxiety may facilitate in that it motivates and is added incentive to keep the student working at the task of preparing for examinations. But, when anxiety becomes too great, it can interfere with the ability to prepare adequately and with a feeling of well-being. In other words, severe anxiety may debilitate the individual from effective activity and adaptation.

In the coming chapters we will discuss the forms of adaptation, the actual approaches the individual utilizes to attack the task *(coping),* and how he controls his feelings so that he may promote his attack upon examinations with utmost effectiveness and success *(defense).*

5

SOME MODES OF
ADAPTATION: COPING

Some General Comments

ADAPTATION, as we have described it, has two basic components: dealing with the situation *(coping)*, and dealing with one's feelings about the situation *(defense)*. As we use these terms they do not involve special personality mechanisms but, rather, constitute the person's whole range of behavior. The severity of stress experienced depends on the number of available means for coping and defense and their efficacy. To the extent that an individual has available effective means for dealing with "possible threat," the situation can be successfully mastered. To the extent that means prove ineffective, stress will increase. As Grinker and Spiegel have noted, "If the threat can be mastered by counteractivity, whether by deception, persuasion, or destruction, anxiety will not arise. Mastery, or its opposite, helplessness, is the key to the ultimate emo-

tional reaction."[1] It is therefore of considerable interest
to understand the institutionalized means available for
dealing with the situation, as well as those that are inno-
vated, and to attempt to ascertain their effectiveness.

The means that may be successful and appropriate in
one situation may not be especially appropriate in some
other, nor will the means appropriate at one point in
time necessarily be effective some time later. The students'
success or failure in coping with examinations is of main
interest, but understanding this requires study of how
these means are learned and adapted, utilized and discarded. Of the effective means some are more structured,
others more idiosyncratic. In this chapter the means most
often employed by the students will be discussed and
some attempt will be made to evaluate them.

Means for Coping

The university graduate department offers structured
means for dealing with examinations that the student,
depending on his perception of what is most necessary for
his preparation, may utilize either maximally or mini-
mally. He can take and audit relevant courses, take specialized reading with a faculty member, review old
examinations, have faculty make recommendations for
reading, and so on. Informally, he may speak with other
students, new and old, have informal discussions with
faculty, and plan studying sessions. Time, however, is
limited, and every student is faced with the problem of
allocating his time in some attempt to find an advanta-
geous approach. He must make some choices concerning
how he will spend whatever time is available to him for

---

1. R. R. Grinker and J. P. Spiegel, *Men Under Stress* (New York:
McGraw-Hill Book Co., Inc., 1945), p. 129.

the purpose of preparation. Approximately one month prior to examinations students were asked to indicate how much time per week during the past month they had spent on each of a number of activities. As the reader can see in Table 14, the students saw themselves as spending the major portion of their working time studying and attending courses. Students also were asked to estimate the total average amount of time they had spent each week during the past month attending courses and studying.

Table 14—Time Spent on Various Activities by Students (Reported Month Prior to Examinations)

Activities	HOURS PER WEEK (PER CENT)					
	Less than 1	1 or 2	3-4	5-7	8-10	11 or more
Bull sessions about examinations	41	46	13	—	—	—
Talking to professors	64	18	18	—	—	—
Studying	—	—	—	18	9	73
Attending courses	—	5	10	33	33	19
Doing research	50	—	18	—	14	18
Leisure time activities	—	—	5	27	14	55

Table 15—Amount of Time Reported by Students Spent Studying and in Courses

Time Spent Studying or in Courses	Number of Students
10 hours or less	1
11-20 hours	2
21-30 hours	6
31-40 hours	7
41-50 hours	4
51 or more hours	2

A considerable time range was reported by students in preparation. Older students, however, reported spending considerably more time studying than did second-year students. Of the eight older students, six were studying 31 or more hours, as compared with only seven of the fourteen second-year students. A similar relationship seemed to hold between level of anxiety and reported amount of time spent in preparation, suggesting that those who felt more threatened, spent more time preparing. The numbers are too small to reach any clear conclusion. It should be recognized, however, that much of the possible result we might have observed was obscured by combining course work and studying, since second-year students had considerably more prescribed course work than older students. This possibly may serve to hide the size of the difference we might have noted if we had considered studying only outside of course work.

Selection of Test Areas

The student's choice of areas is determined in part by factors other than interest, although interest obviously does play a major role. In the early interviews, a number of students reported that in selecting their areas they often considered criteria concerning their ability to perform in these areas, as well as their own interests in the field.

Table 16—Criteria Used in Students' Choice of Optional Areas

Criteria	Per Cent of Students Indicating That the Criterion Was Considered (N-22)
Previous knowledge in areas	86
Whether you had taken courses in the subject	82
Own interests	82
How difficult the various areas were	50
Faculty interests	23
Who was likely to write questions	9
Other	9

We therefore provided students with a check list and asked them which of the indicated criteria they took into account in selecting their optional areas. As one can see in Table 16, factors other than interests were often considered. In some cases students would bypass interests in an area because they could either plan their studying more efficiently or prepare more easily in an area of lesser interest to them.

Techniques of Preparation

Another important aspect of coping concerns the techniques students utilized in preparing for examinations. Both students and faculty were asked to indicate the importance of various practices in preparing for doctoral examinations. The response patterns shown in Table 17

Table 17—Student and Faculty Perceptions of the Importance of Various Practices for Doctoral Examination

Practice	Per Cent of Students Indicating That Practice is Very or Fairly Important	Per Cent of Faculty Indicating That Practice is Very or Fairly Important
Read at least one basic text in each area	100	100
Organize each area around basic ideas and trends	100	100
Review course notes	95	95
Take at least one course in each area	91	77
Read most recent articles in each area	82	86
Go through old examination questions	77	86
Know the biases of faculty members	68	62
Read articles written by faculty members	45	32
Talk to faculty members about the examinations	41	57
Discuss each of the areas with other students	18	50

illustrate the similar distribution of student and faculty attitudes on most items. There was considerable agreement on the part of students and faculty regarding reading relevant texts in each area, reading relevant articles, organizing study around basic ideas and trends, taking courses, and going through old examination questions. Students and faculty differed to a large extent only as to the value of discussing areas with other students. While only 18 per cent of the students thought this valuable, 50 per cent of the faculty thought it important. Also, on the same questionnaire, students and faculty were asked to indicate the importance of talking about examinations to other students who had taken or were taking the examinations. Table 18 indicates the results.

Table 18—Student and Faculty Perception of the Importance of Talking to Other Students About Examinations

	Per Cent of Students Responding Very or Fairly Important (N-22)	Per Cent of Faculty Responding Very or Fairly Important (N-22)
Talking to students who have taken the examinations about the examinations	32	48
Talking to students who are taking the examinations about the examinations	23	43

Although these differences are not very large, the fact that they are both in the same direction of the original finding suggests that the finding was probably not a spurious occurrence. The observed difference in faculty and student perception of the importance of students talking with one another about the examinations was probably attributable to the fact that to some extent the faculty and student orientation and view of the examination process are different. The faculty expect, more than do students, that students will learn from one another, that one of the best means for student stimulation comes from other students. But this ideal picture of the student community is rejected by students who find that they arouse one another's anxiety and feelings of competition. The student, more aware of the practical consequences of communication with his peers, has learned by participation that student communication can have certain disadvantages.

Allocation of Time in Coping

Importance of a studying device is not the sole criterion used by the student in planning his studies. Time is limited, and some studying practices take a great deal more time than others. The student therefore attempts to maintain some useful balance between various preparation devices so that he may use his time in a maximally efficient manner. Students were asked if they had done or intended to do each of a number of things (see Table 19).

Table 19—Use and Intended Use of Studying Devices by Students

Studying Devices	Per Cent of Students Indicating Yes
Review course notes	100
Organize each area around basic ideas and trends	86
Read at least one basic text in each area	82
Take at least one course in each area	64
Read most recent articles in each area	36
Discuss each of the areas with other students	36
Read articles written by faculty members	23

All students do not do everything. Some decision must be made on allocation of time and effort. Reviewing course notes is a method of covering a large range of important material over a short span of time. Also, many students believe that if they know their course material they are bound to pass examinations.

I'm of the opinion that anything which hasn't been treated to some extent in subject matter does not belong on the writ-

tens. . . . That, something, somewhere is wrong if a matter
of crucial importance has not been dealt with at all in class,
and then appears on the writtens. . . . I plan to review all my
notes in the time I have been here. I feel that I will have a
genuine and valid complaint to make if they then presented
material on the writtens which have never been touched on.

This statement might be regarded as a defensive device to
protect the student's feelings about the advisability of his
time allocation in preparation. Whether it is or not, it
does point to the need of the student to make some decisions about how he will restrict his studying. For example,
while 82 per cent of the students felt that reading recent
articles was important, only 36 per cent indicated that
they were doing or intended to do this (see Table 17). In
this situation the studying device, although important, was
very time-consuming and required selection and organization. Thus, most of the students decided that, although
this was important, their time could be better invested in
reading the basic texts that were already organized and
that brought together a great deal of scattered but important materials.

Techniques in Approaching Questions

Prior to examinations most students spend some time
going through old examinations. A month prior to examinations twenty of the twenty-two students under study
reported that they had examined old preliminary examinations. Although fifteen found the experience very or
fairly useful, fourteen of the original students reported
that looking at the old examination questions had made
them anxious. Students who became very anxious when

looking at old examinations did not continue using them very much. This indicates that the students do com-promise between their coping and defense needs.

In talking to old students about the examinations and appraising why it is that those who failed, failed, and those who passed, passed, the student listens to and evalu-ates the various comments he hears. It is this kind of information that leads to the development of strategies about how the examinations should be approached. Al-though the efficacy of these strategies was more strongly believed in by the older students who still were upset about their past failure, all students gave the strategies considerable attention. In the following statements, stu-dents described various strategies for answering questions:

I think he probably tended to write very brief answers and this is not a very appropriate strategy for the examinations. Apparently they prefer you to write . . . lengthy and pedantic sorts of answers and try to bring in all sorts of irrelevant facts. . . . If you want to write what I call pedantic answers, write a lot . . . words themselves, maybe choice of words too, using all sorts of words that are jargon. . . . Make references to as many persons as possible who have contributed to the area and specify their research. If you are discussing research, cite pieces of research, as many as possible, and the contributor, and this sort of thing. In general, include as many details as possible as well as covering the general point.

I've heard many faculty members say [that] the thing to do is to give an answer to the question. The people who have passed have always been the people who would write some-thing regardless of whether they knew the precise answer or not. So that if you have a question you don't know exactly, what you do is distort it into something you do know.

Since a number of strategies were mentioned in the early interviews, both students and faculty were given

a list of strategies and asked to indicate the importance
they attributed to each. Students seemed to feel that strategies were more important than did faculty. In only one case
in Table 20 were faculty more likely than students to
report a strategy as important: that is, where the strategy
itself (writing well-organized answers) required considerable objective ability. The greatest difference of opinion
between students and faculty regarded the strategy of
name-dropping. Students regarded it much more important
than did faculty. Students also believed that citing a great
number of experiments and writing long answers were
important strategies as compared with faculty reports.[2]

Table 20—Student and Faculty Perceptions of the Importance of Examination Strategies

Strategies	Per Cent of Students Reporting Very or Fairly Important	Per Cent of Faculty Reporting Very or Fairly Important
Writing long answers	77	45
Writing well-organized answers	77	100
Using many names	86	41
Citing many experiments	96	73
Making sure you write something for every question	96	86

Table 21—Student and Faculty Reports of the Importance of the Ability to Remember Names, Experiments, and References

Importance	Students (N-22) per cent	Faculty (N-21) per cent
Very important	41	5
Fairly or not very important	59	95

2. One can argue that the proportion of students who view a strategy
as important is not comparable to the proportion of faculty who view this
strategy as important. For example, it may be that if only a small percentage
of powerful faculty members expect something of students, the students
must respond to this. Thus, the fact that at least some faculty members see
each of these strategies as important may mean that students, if they are

Both students and faculty reported that writing something for every question was important.

Since students valued strategies more than faculty, we expected that students might consider the abilities underlying these strategies more important than faculty. Thus, both students and faculty were asked: how important is the ability to remember names, experiments, and references? As Table 21 shows, students reaffirmed, as compared with faculty, that memorization is an important factor in passing examinations. What makes these differences particularly important in student and faculty perception is that they led to consequences which were unanticipated by faculty.

Unanticipated Consequences
of the Examination Situation

We have attempted to indicate how students and faculty to some extent see the process of examinations differently. From the faculty's point of view, one of the major functions of examinations is to encourage intensive study by the student in a number of areas so that he may familiarize himself with a wide range of materials and ideas in the field, and then organize these areas for himself, thereby adding to his maturity as a student and a professional. Thus, it is hoped by the faculty that this experience will be a useful part of the student's training and learning; that through this process he will acquire sophistication and maturity in his chosen field. The examinations also are seen as having a major evaluative

---

to be successful, should use all of these strategies. It appears that using these strategies does help the student's performance.

function, and it is hoped that they will serve as a useful tool for the discrimination of student abilities and potential.

In the student's view, he is asked to prepare for nine two-hour examinations, each in a different area, take courses, work on his Master's thesis, attend to his assistantship obligations, and yet pass these examinations showing an acquired proficiency in understanding the major concepts and ideas in these fields and some mastery of a huge literature. As the student sees it, this is too big a job for any man and he seeks whatever tools are available to make the load lighter.

The examinations themselves are "questionable" instruments for simulating the conditions of scholarship, research, and practice for which the students are being trained. None of these students after leaving graduate school will be completely dependent on memory. A library will be available and, in part, a student's efficacy will depend on how well he can utilize its facilities. Also, his work will rarely necessitate hurried answers; he will have time to reflect, consider, and consult with others. In sum, the conditions imposed upon students by the preliminary written examinations are not necessarily the same conditions his profession will impose upon him in later life.[3]

It is the demanding aspect of examinations that makes it necessary for many students to reject the faculty idea that the examinations represent an intellectual challenge. The student, faced by what he perceives as a serious threat, sees this more as a hurdle he must cope with than as a

---

3. It can be argued that learning would take place more effectively if students studied for and took each of the examinations separately. Having nine examinations in one week is not conducive, particularly, to effective studying or learning.

challenge to his "creative ability" and intelligence.[4] The student, therefore, will adopt those patterns of approach that will best prepare him to meet this threat. Since he has learned from others that experiments and names are important, he will spend hours memorizing these. A number of the students prepared lists of experiments and names for each area which they memorized. Underlying this behavior was the basic idea that there were general research references within the areas that could be dropped in some way, regardless of the questions "they throw at you." Consequently, students had these names and experiments prepared so as to utilize them when the time came. It was generally agreed that past questions had been so vague and general that questions could be turned to one's own devices.

As the examinations approached, the investigator not infrequently saw flash decks that the students were using to learn by rote. They felt that memory was as important a factor in passing examinations as was an understanding of theoretical material and knowledge of the subject matter. Twenty-one of the twenty-two students taking examinations reported that the ability to memorize was either very or fairly important.

The adaptations that students developed to meet the situation were unintended consequences of the preliminary written examination system of the type given in the department studied. And, as this issue is somewhat peripheral to the main topic of the book, this is not the place to pursue it further. What is important for our purposes is to recognize that the observed consequences

---

4. That students do not view the examinations as a challenge to their intelligence and resourcefulness does not mean, necessarily, that intelligence is a minor factor in passing examinations. To this researcher it appears that intelligence and past performance were the best predictors of performance on the examinations.

were related to student techniques of adaptation, and that these techniques were probably functional in terms of the realistic demands of the situation.

A Processual View of Examinations

As examinations drew near, the student's behavior changed considerably. Intensity of study increased, students cut down on recreational activities, and they modified their studying plans as they began to see that their earlier plans were unrealistic. Less effort was devoted to course work and more effort to preparation for examinations. The student began to feel pressed for time; he became more aware of cues and more vulnerable to the effects of social comparison. In short, he began to devote greater energy to his preparation and more concern to his psychological condition. As the frequency of his mood changes increased, he began to have more serious doubts about his abilities and sometimes about his professional goals. His communication concerning examinations increased, and he sought reassurance from others in his group. Joking became more and more frequent, and psychosomatic symptoms began to appear.

Some students became more and more pessimistic; others, as they described it, became "manic" over their feelings of mastery of the material. Dreams about examinations became common, and the examinations began to become the focus of the student's whole life. Some, finding the stress difficult to conquer, obtained tranquilizers to aid them in the last big push; others began to feel hostile and evidences of this hostility began to appear from time to time; still others became involved in magical thinking and behavior. As pessimistic moods set in and as anxiety increased, levels of aspiration were adjusted back and forth, up and down.

A month prior to examinations students were asked to indicate if they had each of a number of experiences. Even a full month prior to examinations these changes were taking place on a large scale. As examinations approached closer and closer these changes became more frequent and intense.

Table 22—Students' Reports of Experiencing Changes as Examinations Approach

Experience	Per Cent of Students Answering Yes (N-22)
Not having enough time to study	95
Increase in amount of studying time	82
Modification of intended reading list	77
A decrease in social and leisure time activities	77
An increase in anxiety over time	73
A decrease in the time and efforts spent on course work	68
An increase in time spent talking about examinations with other students	55
Doubts that going into (field) was the right decision	55
A fairly extensive change in reading plans for examinations	45

These changes in the behavior of students were in part a function of the increased immediacy and saliency of the examinations. They cannot be fully understood, however, until we have discussed to a greater extent the patterns of defense that students develop to deal with their feelings about this oncoming threat. In the next two chapters we will turn to a discussion of defense in the examination situation.

6

SOME MODES OF ADAPTATION: INTERACTIONAL DEFENSE

THE EXAMINATIONS, as we have demonstrated, are a source of considerable discomfort. The student's intense involvement and the importance of the situation to him, as well as competitive interaction, social comparison, and studying, helped maintain his level of anxiety.

Although anxiety can have obvious functions in increasing motivation and effort, it does not always facilitate the student's preparation. In fact, it can be especially detrimental when it becomes too intense and therefore will interfere with the student's studying efforts. Whether or not the added intensity of motivation induced by anxiety can make up for lost efficiency is dependent on the characteristics of the task. On simple and boring tasks anxiety sometimes can lead to an increased over-all efficiency because it may increase motivation. However, when motivation is already high, there is good reason to believe that anxious subjects will perform at an over-all lower level than will nonanxious subjects.[1]

In the group under consideration anxiety sometimes reached so high a level that it clearly interfered with the student's ability to study. The student would find that he could not concentrate and remember the material he was reading. This led to increased concern and what students described as "panic." Realizing that he was acting ineffectively in manipulating the most important and most effective means at his disposal—the ability to study—gave him real reason for concern. The inability to study did become a problem for most students, from time to time, when anxiety became too great, and thus it was very important for them to be able to defend against anxiety.

It appeared that the student who was most effective at studying was the one whose motivation was high but who at the same time was able to control his anxiety. Conversely, some of the students with very little anxiety were hampered in that they did not become sufficiently motivated to study as much as was necessary to perform well on examinations. Thus, the most effective student was able to explore alternatives openly *(cope)* and then to defend when his anxiety level became too great. Defense helped him to contain his anxiety and insulate himself against perceived threat, thus allowing him to continue to cope with some effectiveness.

To recognize the functional character of defense is not to suggest that all of its patterns are effective or desirable. To the extent that defense can lead the person to restrict himself to the point where he avoids useful

---

1. C. D. Smock, "The Relationship Between Test Anxiety, 'Threat-Expectancy' and Recognition Thresholds for Words," *Journal of Personality,* 25, 1956, 191-201.

coping alternatives, excessive defense can become a serious problem. In short, defense, if it is to be effective, should fit the reality demands of the situation. The defense need not necessarily be "true," but it is necessary that it not hamper effective coping techniques.

Faculty not only provided students with information about the examinations and how to prepare for them— studying approaches and methods of organizing materials —but also helped the student to defend against anxiety by reassuring him in various ways. Thus, students frequently interacted with professors to obtain emotional support and reassurance. However, before we can elaborate on how the student's interaction with professors served his defensive needs, it is necessary to discuss briefly somewhat more than we have thus far the department as a system of interacting positions.

Interaction among Students and Professors

As was indicated earlier, graduate students most frequently communicated with the more accessible faculty located in Central Building. Whereas an average of nine students discussed examinations with faculty in Central Building, only an average of two discussed examinations with professors located elsewhere. Since most student-faculty contact occurred within Central Building, the discussion shall be restricted to this context.

Within Central Building, an average of fourteen students communicated with nontenure faculty, whereas only an average of six students communicated with tenure faculty. Thus, although tenure faculty played a greater role than nontenure faculty in the formal training of graduate students, the students associated more frequently and more intensively with the lower-ranking members of the department.

The lesser interaction that tenure professors had with students about examinations suggests that they might not have known these students as well as did the assistant professors, even though they did play the major formal role in graduate teaching. In order to check this possibility, faculty were given a list of students taking examinations and were asked to indicate which of the students they felt they knew well enough to accurately evaluate their abilities and potential. While the assistant professors on the average named fourteen students, the tenure faculty named eleven. Thus, nontenure professors not only interacted more frequently with graduate students but also felt they knew them better.

During the interviews there were various indications that students sought reassurance and support from faculty members. It seems likely, however, that the considerable social distance between students and high-ranking faculty encouraged students to seek support from assistant professors to whom they felt closer. Thus, while the student felt that he could initiate a relationship with an assistant professor primarily for reassurance, this was not sufficient reason to take the time of a high-ranking faculty member.

One may suggest numerous reasons why students felt closer to nontenure than tenure faculty, and various comments by students served to amplify this issue considerably. For one thing, the students perceived nontenure faculty as more supporting because they appeared to be less secure in their positions and future as compared with tenure professors. Also, they, as a group, made a greater attempt than tenure faculty to be friendly to graduate students.

The graduate student represents an important link in communication between younger and older professors. The higher-ranking faculty, with limited opportunity to ascertain how younger staff members are doing in their work, must make evaluations of these younger members in regard to promotion and tenure possibilities. Some of the evaluating evidence, of course, is apparent: rate and quality of publication, research funds from outside agencies, personal impressions in friendly interaction, and the like. However, the tenure professors often know little about how successful or competent a teacher the younger professor may be, and they do not feel free to question the younger faculty member too specifically about his activities, his courses, and so on. Thus the tenure professor must rely primarily on social cues and his impressions through social interaction, realizing that these may be incorrect. Of course, there are occasions when great enthusiasm or dislike for a teacher becomes known through vocal student opinion. But as students usually neither rant nor rave, what and how the assistant professor teaches is mostly his own concern, unknown to others than his students.

Since the persons most familiar with the work of young professors are the graduate students who take their courses, the students, therefore, may have information important but not easily accessible to higher-ranking faculty. And, although higher-ranking faculty usually do not directly solicit evaluations of other professors from graduate students, graduate students often do become a source of such information, and their evaluations do become known to higher-ranking faculty members. Usually this occurs when a high-ranking professor works with and has a good relationship with some student who, in the course of the relationship, begins to feel free enough to make evaluations of other professors, or at least to talk about their attitudes, activities, and so on. Therefore, it is not to the detriment of the career of the assistant professor to develop a good working relationship with graduate students, who are particularly good at rumor-making and rumor-transmission. Also, the assistant professor who can attract good graduate students adds to his own stimulation and research activities. Thus there is some reason to believe that the assistant professor, perhaps not on a level of awareness, does interact down to graduate students with some interest and enthusiasm.

Still another factor in many departments is the social distance between high-ranking and low-ranking faculty members. In many ways it is considerably easier for the young professor to interact effectively with graduate students than with high-ranking faculty. Other factors, too, may account for the intense interaction about examinations between younger faculty members and students. The lower-ranking faculty, often closer to the age group of graduate students than to higher-ranking professors, are often not far enough away from their own experiences as graduate students to have lost the intense graduate student identification. The fact that not too long ago the lower-ranking faculty member has been a graduate student makes it easier for the student to interact with him. Unlike the full professor, he has not yet adopted attitudes fully congruent with the professorial role, although he often may attempt to hide this from his higher-ranking associates. In the following statement a student provides his interpretation for the differences in student communication with nontenure and tenure faculty:

I think it's a function of the faculty members themselves, just how interested they are in interacting with students. . . . I guess because they're closer to it, because it's more recent to them, and they are more sympathetic. . . . The younger people have more recently been students and have not forsaken their identification with students so much, whereas the older people are more fully identified with being faculty members and they just interact among themselves.

Another student explained it this way:

They are more our age-group and have more in common with us socially. . . . [In reference to assistant professors] I think it's part of their assumed role. When you just go into a place, you like to be liked by the students. I see this with [Professor X].

One of the younger faculty members, a recent Ph.D. recipient in the department who was given a temporary staff appointment, described the interaction differences this way:

It looks so damn obvious to me, that I can't really put my finger on it. [Professors A and B] are just not going to spend their time being buddy-buddy with [student Y] or [student Z]. It's just preposterous. It's the way, I guess, as an ex-graduate student that I have come to think of them also. I don't approach them either.

Other factors are also operating within the system that restrict interaction between tenure and nontenure members in the department. Since the tenure faculty member has to evaluate nontenure members, some lack of spontaneity often will appear in these relationships. Often tenure faculty members purposely maintain social distance so that they can feel freer in rendering an adverse decision regarding tenure of the lower-ranking faculty member. Nor does an excessive interaction rate with higher-ranking faculty make a younger professor particularly popular within his peer group.

Status and Reported Interaction

Considerable data have indicated that persons will tend to interact with others of similar social status.[2] When persons interact with others of higher status than they within an organization and when the lower-status persons are in a situation where the higher-status persons have considerable power to affect them, it is likely that they will attend carefully to their interaction with these higher-status persons because of the insecurity of their positions. We predicted, therefore, that when students and faculty did interact, students would attend more carefully to these interactions than would the higher-status faculty members.

Given a list of faculty members, the students were asked to indicate with which faculty members they discussed examinations; faculty members, given the list of students, were asked with which students they discussed examinations. This allowed us to compare student and faculty reports of interaction with the expectation that

Table 23—Discrepancy in Reports of Interaction Between Students and Faculty*

	Number of Faculty Whose Estimates Were Lower Than Reports by Students	Number of Faculty Whose Estimates Were Higher Than Reports by Students	Number of Estimates the Same
Faculty located in Central Building (N-10)	10	0	0
Faculty located in other buildings (N-11)	9	1	1

*One professor refused to report this information.

2. J. Thibaut and H. H. Kelley, *The Social Psychology of Groups* (New York: John Wiley and Sons, Inc., 1959), p. 48.

students would report greater frequency of interaction with faculty than faculty would report with students.

Every faculty member located in Central Building reported less interaction about examinations with students than students reported with them. In buildings outside the Central location, interaction rates, as we showed earlier, were much lower and therefore it should have been easier to remember to whom one spoke. Yet nine of eleven faculty members reported a lower interaction rate with students than students reported with faculty. This result is conservative also since the faculty were asked this question after students had responded, which allowed for a greater period of interaction.[3]

These data suggest that the students find it comforting to communicate with faculty members and that such communication is a way of defending against anxiety. It was therefore predicted that as anxiety increased, so would the

Table 24—Degree of Anxiety and Communication with Faculty Members

Anxiety Groups	CONTACTS WITH PROFESSORS		
	Expected Frequency	Observed Frequency	Mean Number of Students Who Communicated With Faculty
Students with high anxiety (N-7)	35 ⎫	39 ⎫	
	⎬ 70	⎬ 81	5.8
Students with moderate anxiety (N-7)	35 ⎭	42 ⎭	
Students with low anxiety (N-8)	40	29	3.6

3. The assumption was made here that students' reports of interaction with faculty were fairly accurate. If this assumption is rejected, one might argue that students autistically reported interaction that never occurred because it was instrumental to their defense. Another possible explanation of this result is that students may have communicated with faculty about examinations without making it clear that their question pertained to examinations. If this was the case it might explain the discrepancy in reports between faculty and students. However, this latter explanation still cannot possibly explain our subsequent findings on the perception of social association with faculty members.

need to communicate with faculty members. The relationship between experiencing anxiety and reported communication with faculty members about examinations is shown in Table 24. As examination of the table shows, there was a slight difference opposite from the predicted direction between the high- and moderate-anxiety students. However, persons of high and moderate anxiety in Table 24 did communicate more about examinations with professors than did students of low anxiety.

There are possible alternative explanations for the results reported in Table 24. For one thing, older students, who are more anxious than second-year students, have been in the department for a longer period and therefore would know more professors and find it easier to communicate with them. Since our sample is too small to check this notion, no statistical information is available. However, the interviews with students do suggest that anxiety was the important variable that accounted for the communication rate with faculty. Another possible hypothesis to explain this result is that since more persons taking area 1 as their specialty were high-anxiety persons, and, since there were more professors in area 1 than in other areas, this might explain the difference. But the correctness of this hypothesis seems unlikely since area of specialization was not a significant factor affecting interaction between students and professors, and also because professors in area 1 were not those most often communicated with by students.

If our hypothesis is correct—that persons in insecure status positions attend more carefully to their interactions with higher-status persons than do the high-status persons —we might also have suspected that students would find it comforting to see themselves as social friends of the faculty, since this would serve their defensive needs and add to their security. We therefore asked students to indicate which of the faculty members they associated with socially, and asked faculty members to indicate which of the students they associated with socially. While the question asked of both groups was the same, it was predicted that students would interpret the word "socially" differently from professors, and that they would report more associations with faculty members than would the faculty.

Table 25—Perception of Social Associations by Students and Faculty in Central Building

Professorial Rank	Number of Students Named by Faculty (1)	Number of Students Naming Faculty Members (2)	Difference 1-2
Tenure professors			
Professor 1	0	0	0
Professor 2	0	0	0
Professor 3	0	0	0
Professor 4	0	0	0
Professor 5	0	2	2
Professor 6	0	1	1
Assistant professors			
Professor 7	1	6	5
Professor 8	3	10	7
Professor 9	12	1	—11*
Professor 10	0	0	0†

*The professor who listed twelve students qualified his listing by the comment "only in a limited way."
†Visiting professor for one semester.

While very few social relationships were reported, especially among tenure professors and students, there was a tendency for students to perceive relationships which faculty reports did not indicate. For example, although no tenure faculty member reported interacting socially with any student, three such relationships were reported by students with tenure faculty members. When we move to the assistant professor level, both students and faculty reported such relationships. The reason for this difference is that as there is more interaction between students and assistant professors, the students could more easily assume "social friendship." Although perception often is based on wishful thinking, as many social psychological studies have shown, a healthy defense does require some realistic cues on which to base an estimate. Since, as was pointed out earlier, there is much more communication between students and assistant professors, there was a more realistic basis for perceiving oneself as a social associate of the assistant professor. In the case of professors 7 and 8, sixteen social relationships were reported by students; only four of these were reciprocated. Professor 9, presenting a strange reversal, modified his report by an attached note indicating that he was a social associate of the twelve students he named "only in a very limited way." This professor was the newest member of the department's full-time staff. As the student quoted earlier remarked of professors, "When you go to a place you like to be liked by the students." He then had mentioned the behavior of professor 9 as an example. Thus, the results show that there was a tendency for the student to report more social relationships with faculty than vice versa. If we omit professor 9, we find that, while students reported fifteen such relationships in the Central Building, faculty reported only four such relationships. Considering the entire group of students, this is not a particularly strong, or a practically significant defense. But it is supporting evidence of the earlier finding reported that persons in lower-status positions are more attentive to their interactions with higher-status persons than are higher-status persons with persons in lower social positions.

From the point of view of defense, we would also suspect that the perception of the power of faculty members would be influenced by rate of association and, also, that powerful professors would be perceived as more benevolent than less powerful professors. In a relevant study, Pepitone[4] found that subjects would attribute friendliness to judges who had the most power to decide whether they would receive a prize. To what extent did the students under stress perceive professors in a similar way?

Students were asked to indicate which faculty members they thought had most power in the department, the least power, would be most likely to support their position if they performed marginally, and could be least expected to support their position if they performed marginally. They were also asked with which faculty members they felt most closely associated, and which would be most instrumental in making a decision about them.

Faculty members who were named three or more times as high-power persons, and no more than three times as low-power persons, were treated as high-power members of the faculty. This group included nine professors, eight of them from the Central Building. The mean number of times these persons were named as high-power was 7.8; the mean number of times these persons were named as low-power was .8. The low-power group included twelve members of the faculty. The mean number of times this group was rated as high-power was .3; the mean number of times they were rated as low-power was 4.8.

There are some interesting points about the power ratings. For example, the high-power group included two assistant professors, both of whom were rated as higher power than one of the full professors who was rated as low power.

When students were asked to name professors who were most likely to support their positions, high-power professors were named forty-five times, an average of five times

4. A. Pepitone, "Motivational Effects in Social Perception," *Human Relations, 3,* 1950, 57-76.

each; low-power professors, twenty-three times, an average of 1.9 times each. On the other hand, when students were asked to name professors least likely to support their positions, there was almost no difference between the two groups; professors rated as high power were named thirteen times for a mean of 1.4, while professors rated as low power were named fifteen times for a mean of 1.3. Also, when the question was asked about supporting choices, faculty were named sixty-eight times. When names were requested for nonsupporting faculty, they were named only twenty-eight times.

Table 26—Student Perception of Faculty Power and Support*

| | MEAN NUMBER OF FACULTY NAMED | |
	Who Would Support Students' Positions	Who Would be Least Likely to Support Students' Positions
Faculty rated as high power (N-9)	5.0	1.4
Faculty rated as low power (N-12)	1.9	1.3

*The twenty-second member of the faculty, the student who had become an instructor, was not included in the obtained ratings.

The student also was asked who he thought would be most instrumental in making a decision about him at the final faculty meeting. Faculty rated as high power were named more often than those rated as low-power faculty; the average number of times high-power faculty were named was 5.4, while the average for low-power faculty was 1.3 times. The assistant professor having the highest interaction rate with students and who had been rated high power by students was seen as more instrumental in decision-making by students than all but one of the other members of the department. Only one other professor, who of the tenure professors had the highest interaction rate with students, was named more often as instrumental than the assistant professor under discussion. It is interesting that this assistant professor told many of the students that they had nothing to worry about, that "they had it made." And, in reward for the confidence he placed in them, he was attributed with power and influence, which, of course, he did not really have.[5] A second assistant professor who was new in the department and very friendly to students was seen more often as instrumental in making a decision about students than were four of the tenure professors. The third assistant professor, seen more often as instrumental than were three of the tenure professors, was considered as instrumental as a fourth tenure professor. Thus, although students were careful with their estimates of power, autistic perception did play a greater role in judging instrumentality and influence, and lower-ranking faculty members who interacted frequently with students were attributed considerable instrumentality. At best this was wishful thinking, for, as we will later show, tenure faculty members were those who spoke most at the final faculty meeting, and who also made the most remarks of a positive or negative nature. When assistant professors spoke about students, their comments, more often than not, were neutral.

In the data presented thus far, there is one point that, although not obvious, is vastly important. In looking at the perception of power and instrumentality, in the latter case the autistic effect can be more clearly detected. This, we think, is not a fortuitous happening. To perceive assistant professors as having more power than full professors is clearly autistic, and is likely to receive little environmental or social support. However, instrumentality judgments do allow a wide range of criteria, and attribution

5. The data were discussed with this particular assistant professor. He found it surprising and amusing that students attributed so much instrumentality to him, which, he frankly admitted, was nonexistent.

of instrumentality to an assistant professor can receive realistic support in the form of cues from the environment, knowledge that assistant professors know some students more thoroughly than full professors, and so on. The student, in other words, can find some rational basis for making the judgment and this comforting perception may in fact have some environmental support, as in the case of the assistant professor who told students that they "had it made."

At the risk of being repetitive, let us emphasize that defense—even "unconscious defense"—need not be "correct" or "incorrect," "healthy" or "unhealthy." What is important is that the defensive technique does not become too unique or too unusual. As long as there is some realistic basis for doubt, a misperception based on some information may be comforting and useful.

We now move to a second chapter on modes of defense. In the coming chapter we will deal with a variety of reports that students made of their interactions with others, as well as their reports about their own thought processes.

7

SOME MODES OF
ADAPTATION: DEFENSE

IN PRECEDING CHAPTERS we have already said a good deal concerning interactional and cognitive modes of defense. In this chapter defense processes will be approached in a more systematic fashion. As we see it, a person's behavior represents a more or less consistent pattern of response—what we call his *personality*. He attempts to maintain cognitive integration by controlling the information that enters the cognitive system and by making it congruent with his views and needs.[1]

Organizing his behavior around attitudes of the self and the relations of the self to the external world, he deals not only with objective situations, but also with perceived subjective threats. The information that enters the cognitive system may be relevant or irrelevant, im-

1. Leon Festinger, *A Theory of Cognitive Dissonance* (Evanston: Row, Peterson and Company, 1957).

portant or unimportant to the task at hand or to the attitudes the person holds about himself in relation to the task. In instances where relevant information does enter the system, the individual may either integrate it into his cognitive orientation or attempt to reject it. In doing this he seeks various kinds of support from others in the communication structure of which he is a part and from cues which he finds in his environment.

The system of defenses described by the classical psychoanalytic theorists attempts to indicate *what* occurs, but tells us little that is clear as to *how* this occurs. Thus, whereas the descriptions of behavior—repression, denial, projection, intellectualization, and so on—sensitize us to these happenings, the conditions under which these distortions occur and how they develop remain unclear.

A step in the direction of solving this problem has been provided by some interesting studies by David Hamburg and his associates.[2] Studying the adaptive processes of badly burned soldiers, they observed that many of the adaptive processes were social—that these processes involved communication as well as cognition, and that cognitive defenses were associated with environmental cues. These insightful papers suggested that perhaps we might learn a good deal more if we would attempt to understand the social and social-psychological contexts within which defense occurs.

The Need for Defense

The students under study most definitely saw stress as a major factor in the challenge of passing the examinations. Many of them believed that if they could defend

---

2. D. Hamburg, Beatrix Hamburg, and S. deGoza, "Adaptive Problems and Mechanisms in Severely Burned Patients," *Psychiatry, 16,* 1953, 1-20.

adequately and maintain their anxiety at some comfortable level, they would be adequate in their performance. Both students and faculty were asked to indicate the importance of the ability to remain relaxed and the ability to work under pressure for students taking preliminary examinations. The difference in perception of stress as a factor was quite considerable when viewed through the eyes of students and faculty in Table 27.

Table 27—Perceived Importance of Defending Against Stress by Students and Faculty

Items	Per Cent of Students Responding Very or Fairly Important (N-22)	Per Cent of Faculty Responding Very or Fairly Important (N-21)
Ability to remain relaxed	68	29
Ability to work under pressure	100	76

Table 28—Rated Importance of the Ability to Put Aside Everything for Studies by Students and Faculty

	Per Cent Responding Very or Fairly Important
Students (N-22)	91
Faculty (N-21)	38

Since, as indicated in the last chapter, students do find that preparation is a major factor in reducing anxiety, tasks that keep them from working on examination preparation were likely to raise their anxiety level. We expected, therefore, that students would think it more important than faculty to put aside everything for their studies in order to pass the examinations. And, as analysis of Table 28 shows, they did just this.

Comforting Cognitions and Favorable Social Comparison

The most consistently observed defense device used by the students under study was that of seeking comforting information from the environment that was consistent with the attitudes and hopes the student held about the examinations. Often these comforting cognitions were made on the basis of comparing oneself favorably with others, or by finding cues in the environment that made the person more confident about his situation. A number of these comforting cognitions have already been pointed to in preceding chapters. For example: "most students who had failed preliminary examinations in the past had had difficult personalities"; "the faculty expects less from this year's group as compared with earlier ones because most of the people in the present group have been here for only two years."

This is not to say that what is necessarily comforting for one student is comforting for all. But in general the persons who most often verbalized these attitudes were those for whom they were most comforting as measured by other criteria. For example, as we have pointed out, the attitude concerning the faculty expecting less of second-year students was developed and communicated by second-year students. It is true that one or two of the older students also accepted this idea, but these students had little to lose by its acceptance. In addition, the fact that a belief may be accurate does not invalidate it as a defense; on the contrary, accurate beliefs are valuable as defenses because they do have environmental support. Thus, while the inaccurate defenses may be more striking to the observer, they are probably more likely to lead to later problems of adaptation. The student who can draw satisfaction from the fact that he is competent and that others think him competent is in a better position than the student who holds this as an illusion.

A number of comforting thoughts, verbalized in early interviews with the students, were included in the questionnaire administered to students. They were asked to indicate how often they had felt, thought, said, or done each of a number of things (see Table 29).

Table 29—Students' Reported Use of Comforting Cognitions

Comforting Cognitions	PER CENT OF STUDENTS	
	Who Report Using This Cognition Very or Fairly Often	Who Report Using These Cognitions With any Frequency
I'm as bright and knowledgeable as other students who have passed these examinations	64	91
I've handled test situations in the past—there's no good reason why not now	59	86
I am doing all I can to prepare—the rest is not up to me	50	86
I wouldn't have gotten this far unless I knew something	50	86
I'm well liked in this department	45	77
I've already demonstrated my competence on past work, they will pass me	26	77
You can't fail these examinations unless you really mess up	23	73
They wouldn't fail me—they've already decided I'm going to pass	18	30
This is a test of stress; I can deal with that	14	59
If I'm not cut out for the field, it's best that I know it now	14	55

The assurance that occurred most frequently resulted from favorable social comparison—a student compared himself with other students who had taken examinations in prior years and passed, and told himself that he was as knowledgeable or more so than the student with whom he was comparing himself. Others *drew on past experience,* and, by reassuring themselves of their competence in the past, they felt more competent in the present: "I wouldn't have gotten this far unless I knew something," "I've handled situations in the past," and other such similar statements. Still others saw themselves as well liked, and almost all of the students believed to some extent that if you were liked, your chances of having a good outcome on the examinations were better. Others sought to externalize responsibility: "If I am doing all I can, what's the use of worrying?" Let us take some examples from the interviews to illustrate how the student verbalized these comforting comparisons and cognitions.

I think I'll pass because I think that if decisions have been made previously, that I'm one who will pass rather than fail. . . . So I'll really have to botch up writtens to get them to alter their opinion of me. . . . I evaluate the people on the faculty as being reasonable people . . . who should make reasonable demands for performance on writtens which I should be able to meet.

[I was saying] that we are pretty scared of the questions that were asked on the old examinations and yet we haven't seen the answers that people have given to these questions to see what they were like; to see the quality of the answers—the answers which were acceptable in terms of passage. Perhaps, if we were able to see some of the answers that have been acceptable, we would feel a little better. I don't feel that we are significantly more defective than other people who have passed these . . . or that we worked any less. From this standpoint, it would seem that our chances of passing are just as good as those who passed.

I was afraid that reading so few books wouldn't be enough. Then I found out that other people were reading these and felt secure with them. Now I feel better.

It seems that people pass [the examinations] pretty easily.

I have a much better memory than most people.

[I tell] myself how clever I am. . . . I usually have done better. I think it contributes to my normal state of well-being.

Considering the people who passed previously, I think my chances are at least even.

Hundreds of such statements came up in the interviews with students. The examples took many forms, and enumerating them would be unnecessary for our argument. What is important to recognize is that these beliefs arose in the interaction process; they were exchanged back and forth among students, and many were held commonly and were consensually validated.

This is not to suggest that all social comparisons are favorable. As we indicated earlier, social comparison often aroused anxiety. It is through social comparison processes that the individual attempts to ascertain both his strengths and his weaknesses and to evaluate what soft spots need plugging. The student who fails to take part in this type of social comparison can lose considerable information about the examinations and possible modes of preparation, although as a result he may be able to keep his anxiety at a lower level. This was especially true of two low-anxiety isolated students who were not comparing themselves to others, and who had little idea how much others were studying. Both of these students studied considerably less than the rest of the group, and both performed at a level below the expectations of faculty. One of these two students had communicated and compared himself so little with others, that he had no idea that other students were aiming to pass at the Ph.D. level. All along, he prepared casually, feeling that he would be satisfied attaining an M. A. pass. After the examinations the student became considerably agitated about his performance, knowing that had he set his expectations higher he might have performed better and closer to the expectations others had of him. The reactions of these two low-anxiety persons were somewhat similar to the reactions that Grinker and Spiegel observed among some soldiers: "One sometimes sees men who err in the opposite direction and fail to interpret danger when they should. As a consequence, they are protected against developing subjective anxiety. . . . The defect in discrimination gives them the appearance of being unrealistic and slap-happy, illustrating the maxim that fools walk where angels fear to tread."[3]

It is thus the process of social comparison that allows the student to pace himself. For example, one student decided a few weeks prior to examinations to postpone them until the following fall. Notice how social comparison was a prime influence in this decision.

I think, to a great degree, interacting with people like you who keep asking me what I am doing and other people who are doing things, sort of hearing that certain people are reading this, that, and the other, has kind of gotten me to the point of feeling that I'm not preparing for them like other people are. I really don't have a chance to. Maybe it would be best that I didn't take them at all rather than take them and not do so well. . . . I talked to a couple of people, [student X] and [student Y], in Central Building, and I've heard some from my office partner who knows [students A, B, and C] who are taking them and he related some of the things that they are doing. I feel, myself, that I would like to do some of these things . . . I don't have the time this semester. . . . So these sorts of things have gotten me to think that I'm not preparing too well. And I think that it would be best that I don't take them at all.

Joking and Humor

Joking as a useful form of defense has been given considerable attention by philosophers, psychologists, and humorists, but only in recent years have its social func-

---

3. R. R. Grinker and J. P. Spiegel, *Men Under Stress* (New York: McGraw-Hill Book Co., Inc., 1945), p. 128.

tions been noted to any significant degree. In recent studies by Coser, Fox, and Hamburg and associates on the hospital ward,[4] some of the social functions of joking under stress have been pointed out.

Four weeks prior to examinations students were asked to indicate how much they joked about examinations. Every student indicated that he had joked to some extent.

Table 30—The Extent of Student Joking About Examinations

Extent of Joking	Per Cent of Students (N-22)
Joked a great deal	23
Joked some	54
Joked not very much	23
Joked none	—

Table 31—Student Status and Joking

	JOKED		
	A Great Deal	Some	Not Very Much
	Per Cent	Per Cent	Per Cent
Older students (N-8)	—	62	38
Second-year students (N-14)	36	50	14

The older students who were more anxious and more upset about examinations seemed to find it more difficult to find humor in the examination situation.

Since joking is an interpersonal event and may serve as an avoidance device in interaction, we would expect that joking about examinations would be more likely to arise among the second-year students, who are more centrally located in the communication structure, than among those more isolated. Table 32 confirms this.

It appears that joking occurred primarily among those who were high-moderate and moderate-anxiety types. Stu-

4. Rose L. Coser, "Some Social Functions of Laughter," *Human Relations*, *12*, 1959, 171-182; Renée Fox, *Experiment Perilous* (New York: The Free Press of Glencoe, 1959); Hamburg *et al.*, *op. cit.*, p. 5.

Table 32—Joking Among Second-Year Students and Centrality in the Communication Structure*

Degree of Centrality	JOKED		
	A Great Deal	Some	Not Very Much
	Per Cent	Per Cent	Per Cent
Three or more communication links (N-6)	67	33	—
Less than three communication links (N-8)	12	63	25

*This relationship did not hold among older students. Having three or more communication links was atypical of older students.

dents who were very anxious, with some exceptions, did not see the examinations as humorous as did some of the moderate-anxiety students. This was true especially of the older students who felt that they had suffered considerably in going through the process; yet it did appear that humor was an important mode of anxiety reduction. Also it seemed that joking occurred most frequently at certain points in time. For example, it seemed to increase in intensity just prior to the week of examinations, and the form that it took also seemed to change. Well before examinations, joking consisted mainly of poking fun at the material—a form of tension release. As examinations approached, however, tension-release humor still was present, but avoidance banter seemed to increase in significant quantity. A possible explanation for the change in the kind of joking forms was that as the examinations approached, time pressures increased and students became aware that time for future coping effort was limited. Therefore, a useful defense would allow for avoidance of serious discussion about examinations and avoidance of the kinds of anxiety stimuli that were discussed in an earlier chapter. For example, a few days prior to examinations, it would be of little use for a student to discover that five important textbooks had been read by others while he had spent his time on less significant details. Joking as an avoidance technique allowed for keeping further information that might have been disruptive out of one's frame of reference.

Before going on to describe and give some examples of the kinds of humor that developed, the reader should be warned that he might not find student humor terribly humorous. Humor is highly situational and often specific to those sharing a common frame of reference. Regardless of how the jokes appear to the reader, they were in fact funny from the student's perspective.

JOKING AS A FORM OF TENSION RELEASE. Joking is a useful device to reduce tensions resulting from uncertainty. One of the more common problems for students in dealing with examinations is the uncertainty they feel as to which questions or areas will appear on examinations and the sampling used in choosing these questions. Students feel that it is conceivable that one can know an area well yet encounter an examination where he cannot answer the questions. Put in another way, students believe that an element of chance is operating, that the student may be lucky or unlucky in the questions he encounters. In the student story that follows, the uncertainty in the examination process was made to appear ludicrous.

I heard a cute story the other day about the manner in which certain people go around assigning questions for the examinations. . . . He grabs down a great big book and goes thumbing through it and happens to pick up one little area, one little section in the bottom of the page in the middle of the volume. And he says: "Hmmmm, this strikes my fancy. I've never seen this before. I think I'll put this on the examinations and see what they could tell me about this."

One of the situations found most amusing by the students concerned a discussion about a possible question on

examinations. As the reader will remember, most of the
students felt that if you do not know the answer to a question, you still should attempt to write something. The
situation described below deals with a discussion of this
strategy.

When I walked into the Monday class, everyone was joking
around . . . [student *D*] was telling us his point of view of
what he would do if he didn't know a question. . . . He would
give another answer to it. . . . The other fellows said, "Okay,
we'll test you out. What is the [Spencer] hypothesis?" or some
obscure thing I never heard of. And so [student *D*] sort of
laughed and said, "Well, I never heard of that but I'm sure
getting familiar with the [Zipp] effect."

[Later student *D*] came in and said, "Okay, I found out what
[Spencer] is." And [student *A*], who doesn't take our other
course, said, "WHAT???" And everybody said, "You better be
sure you know that, that's very important." And someone said
it was such and such and such. And somebody else turned
around and said, "What is its present status?," and everybody
laughed.

Here again, the question, "What is its present status?"
was experienced by the group as a humorous remark. This
is probably due to the fact that many of the questions on
doctoral examinations ask students to discuss the development and present status of various concepts. In a sense the
group was having a good laugh over the examinations and,
to some extent, over the stereotyped forms the questions
sometimes take.

Another source of humor was the obscure items that
students often pick up in their reading for examinations,
that they then go around and jokingly ask other students
about. In a sense this represents a take-off on the anxiety-
arousing effect students have on one another, and also is

sometimes used as a device to hide one's own anxiety about examinations. Below are some examples:

Generally we joke about things that don't mean too much . . . and obscure things. [Student *F*] said something like, did I know that the average visual acuity of an eight-year-old elephant was the same as a female horse?

He came across a little bit about Meyer, the photosensitive crab. So this seemed like a particular bit of nonsensical information which he passed all over the department. "You got to know about Meyer." It has kind of been the joke of the week.

One of the students who participated a great deal in joking described what he perceived to be the function of joking about examinations.

All of this doesn't mean anything. It's not going to be useful in preparing for the writtens . . . but I think it's a tension-reducing mechanism. It keeps you from getting too serious about them, in a sense, letting the thing get the better of you, which I'm sure has happened to some people in the past, and I'm sure it has had an adverse effect.

Students also made seemingly silly comments to one another, or thought of funny comments they might make. Apparently this made the whole process seem a little more unreal, a little less serious.

I was thinking about walking in on the first examination and yelling, "Hey, I thought this was going to be multiple choice."

"SICK" HUMOR. This type of humor is represented by jokes about failing. Usually these jokes involve saying, "I'm going to fail, ha, ha, ha," or "We'll fail and then we can go out and kill ourselves." By attaching an absurdity to the situation, the student seemed to make the real situation and the threat it presented more remote and more impossible.

Another kind of "sick" humor pertained to what the student should do should he fail. Once again the same function was apparent. By making the possibilities absurd, failure seemed more remote.

[Student *C*] said, "Next year at this time, I'll be getting ready to get out of this place, and I'll be looking for a job." And I said, "Yeah, next year at this time I might be selling shoes." Someone else said, "Yeah, if it weren't for these writtens."

We got into a discussion, you know, how I always wanted to sell shoes. . . . A lot of talk is this sort of humorous thing about it.

Whether the jokes were concerned with selling shoes or picking cotton, their intent was the same: to debunk the seriousness of the possible outcomes. This could take various forms; for example, one student usually referred to the examinations as the "spring quizzes."

JOKING AS AN AVOIDANCE DEVICE. Joking is one of the most effective methods for avoiding a serious discussion. Certainly anyone who has ever tried to have a serious discussion with a person who insists on being jovial will realize how effective humor may be as an avoidance device. It allows an individual to fend others off in a friendly but effective fashion, and it makes them keep their distance. It also can be used as a form of attack on others, and should they object, one always can have the recourse to "I was only joking." It is this ambiguous function of joking that allows one to attempt attack and avoidance without making himself too vulnerable to being charged with his offense. One student explained how joking might be utilized in this fashion:

When [student X] comes in, he wants to talk seriously about the examinations. But I don't want to talk seriously about them because I feel that I'm not going to pass and that isn't very funny. Another thing is that I don't want to tell him that I don't think I'm going to pass. . . . [Student X], he's pretty serious and I tease him. He comes in and asks, "What are you studying for statistics?" And I spend the next five minutes reeling off all this nonsense (laughs), and he's getting more and more anxious. He just bothers most people more because he is serious. He's pretty anxious really. . . . Everybody is just real childish and real silly. It's easier to be funny than to be serious.

The joking playfulness one can observe here combined teasing, hostility, and anxiety avoidance. One student, for example, related how he became very anxious after he had found a question he could not answer on an old examination. After asking another student if he knew the answer, he reported that the other student also became anxious, and, feeling that he had done his duty, he went to bed. Another student, from the viewpoint of the recipient of the communication, related a somewhat similar situation:

When I try to study in the office, somebody will come up to me and say, "What are you studying? What are you studying?" When I tell them, they say, "Oh, you don't want to study that. What do you want to study that for?" And they'll go on. It makes me angry. They're doing it because they feel threatened sort of. . . . Everyone wants to be sure that nobody knows anything more than they do. . . . So instead you tease.

One student who generated considerable anxiety, and who a number of students were avoiding, was sometimes heavily sanctioned by names. This was done to discourage his serious attitude toward examinations, which made the other students anxious.

Students also did a considerable bit of clowning.

[Student *B*] was on a jag a couple weeks ago. Every time someone walked into the room, he asked them, "Why are you so hostile to me?". . . . It's just easier to keep laughing. It doesn't bother you as much to joke about it.

This kind of joking, especially among one of the cliques, continued until writtens began, and then to some extent seemingly subsided. At any rate, there was an apparent decrease in the hostile jabbing that had taken place just before the examinations. Once examinations started, however, students became more genuinely friendly to one another and supported one another more than they had at any prior period. It would appear that once the examinations had begun, and some of the tension was reduced, the competitive jockeying was no longer necessary. The clearly defined threat now was not other students but the examinations themselves. And the group seemed to unite against this threat. The details of this, however, shall be left for a later chapter.

Seeking Comforting Cues

As has already been indicated on a number of occasions, students are very sensitive to cues related to the impending examinations and to their prestige in the department. Seeking these cues from many available sources, they attribute at times considerable importance to what are often unimportant and casual comments made by faculty members. However, the students themselves are aware of their tendency to autistically perceive cues, and, when they find themselves doing this to extremes, they often attempt to control it. Some cues, however, do have sound bases, and students seek cues on which they can base the beliefs they develop. Below are some examples:

I feel pretty confident of my grasp of the material at this point. . . . Also, the little signs of encouragement for my applying to [job] . . . which has a fairly good reputation. They wouldn't have encouraged me to apply there unless they felt that I was doing fairly well. . . . Also, my appointment this year. I perceive this as positive feedback. . . . There's sort of a predetermined hierarchy of values, and I guess this is second only to the [x] stipends.

[Professor Y] called me in and he said that he wanted to be sure that I wanted to do my dissertation in his area. And that was real nice. . . . He had to assume I was going to pass in order to talk this way at all, but I could sort of detect, you know, sort of a vote of confidence that the people think I'm going to pass. Everybody thinks so. . . . I talked to [Professor Y] for a while and he thinks that I'm going to pass. He thinks that it's a riot that I'm so sad. . . . He laughs, "You don't need to study. You can handle the questions; chuck them away."

As examinations approached and there was little more that the student could do, reassurances were accepted more readily; it was during this period that cues were most often perceived. Early in the preparation period, when student motivation was still important, faculty reassurances had been more likely to be rejected, for fear that they might interfere with the motivation to prepare adequately. One of the students, who found reassurances very comforting in the later period, was rather critical of them in the early preparation period.

They are a little bit too far away from [the examinations]. Like one of them who says, "Just assume you're going to pass." You know, that's a little hard to make when 50 per cent didn't on the last round. It's a little incongruent with what actually happened.

Cues, however, are not always perceived favorably. One

student went into a rather intense depressive mood prior to examinations. In investigating the source of this depression, it was discovered that in talking with a faculty member, he had expressed his anxieties and indicated that he was worried that if he did not pass the examinations, he would not be able to get a job. The faculty member had responded that there were many jobs that he could get if he did not pass. The student perceived that this comment meant that the faculty were expecting to fail him and that this was why he was being told that he could find a number of jobs if he failed examinations. This inaccurate perception initiated a rather severe depression. Thus, extrasensitivity to faculty cues sometimes did become a burden. In short, although most faculty cues were interpreted favorably, there were occasions where an unfavorable interpretation initiated considerable anxiety.

Sometimes faculty members evoked unintended cues that upset the student, for, as we have shown, the faculty is not as sensitive to faculty-student interaction as is the student. One of the older students, for example, reported that a faculty member had asked him on the night before taking an examination if he had read a particular book in this professor's area. Consequently, the student stayed up all night reading this book, assuming that a question on the examination would be based on it, and went into the examination without any sleep. There were no questions concerning the book on the examination.

Indeed, the students' sensitivity to cues is an interesting phenomenon. Similar kinds of behavior probably occur in other such situations where major rewards are at stake. In the section on the student's behavior before learning the results of his examination performance, we shall return to a further discussion of cues.

Mastery

As the examinations approached, the students began to get evidence of having attained some mastery over the materials they had been studying. Mastery is objectively indicated by the student's realization that he now can handle questions on old examinations that he was not able to handle earlier. Also, many of the students found that as examinations drew near, the experience did not seem nearly as bad as they had expected and they found comfort in the fact that they were defending so adequately.

If I can go over some material that I've looked over a month ago, and show pretty good mastery of it, then my spirits go up and I feel more confident.

Now I'm getting to feel that it's sort of a possibility that you can answer the questions and I think my anxiety has generally decreased.

I think, in general, that I adapted to the examination situation better than I anticipated. I was sure that I was going to approach a psychotic break or at least be on tranquilizers for three months prior to examinations. None of this has been necessary. . . . Previously, every time somebody would drop a name, I would get very anxious. Now I'm beginning to realize [talking to others] can be quite helpful, so I'm beginning to do this. Instead of avoiding the issue like I did before, I guess I'm meeting more than I did before.

Being a Member
of a Select Group

Members of one of the cliques on the main communication link spoke a great deal about being a member of a select group (the second-year group). A similar feeling of

cohesion under stressful circumstances was reported also
by Grinker and Spiegel.[5] Comments such as the following
were frequently made:

We are the first group that has been admitted here that has
stuck so long as a group. We haven't lost anybody and we have
been here for two years now. There is a sense of group unity
which these people are trying to identify with more strongly.
. . . I know that I have felt a number of times that I am part
of a group that is considered to be an exceptionally good
group. So, essentially, there shouldn't be too much to worry
about.

Magical Practices

The most unusual of the defense devices that occurred
among a number of students, also reported by Grinker
and Spiegel[6] among combat troops, were superstitious,
compulsive, magic-like practices. Students, however, recognized the superstitious characteristics of their behavior.
Nonetheless this behavior persisted, although its functions
are not too clear. They may have made the student feel
that he had control over the situation, while at the same
time he externalized responsibility.

If I was going to pass, then I was going to fail. And if I was
going to think that I was going to fail terribly, maybe, somehow, it was going to change around the other way. I wouldn't
even consciously entertain the idea that I was going to pass.

The morning of the first examination we woke up. . . . and
we found this string with a letter attached to it so that you
couldn't help but see it. And we opened the letter and it was
from [older student, *T*]. And it was satirical and so forth,

5. Grinker and Spiegel, *op. cit.*
6. *Ibid.*

"Yea, thou walks through the valley of writtens." . . . He enclosed three red rocks in the envelope saying that these were good-luck charms. All three of us kept them with us throughout the examinations. It was almost a fetish. We had to. And I remember the first day, I lost mine. I lost it before going to examinations and it was late. And I knew I had put it somewhere, but I didn't remember where. And I was getting panicked. I kept running around the house trying to find the little rock. And, as it was, I couldn't find it and I came to examinations ten minutes late because I was looking for the rock . . . I realized how superstitious and idiotic this was, and yet I still persisted. When I found the rock, I was really overjoyed. I kept it with me the rest of the examinations. This was superstitious behavior I thought I would never engage in, but it's funny what you will do when you're under stress.

The most frequently engaged in magic-like thought processes were similar to the one described by the student who felt that he must not think that he was going to pass. This thought is somewhat similar to that of the combat troops who purposely miscounted their number of flying hours.[7] Students were careful not to think or at least not to verbalize arrogant and superior thoughts, for this was seen as tempting one's own downfall. One function for this kind of behavior is not very obvious: the student who thinks and acts humbly usually presents a picture to others that he is humble. Students felt, as an earlier quote indicated, that there was good reason to believe that they were expected to be somewhat upset about examinations. Not only was there a feeling that a cocky attitude would bring faculty retaliation, but many rumors of events seemed to substantiate this concept. For example, when both students and faculty were presented with this statement, "The faculty is favorably impressed by persons

7. *Ibid.*

who seem anxious about examinations," 77 per cent of the students attributed some truth to it, while 68 per cent of the faculty agreed. Obviously there was some faculty support for this feeling.

The compulsive magic-like thinking seemed to occur more frequently among the better students than among the poorer ones. The latter, bothered by feelings that they were going to fail, often attempted to reassure themselves with favorable indications. It may be that this magical thought among the better students served as a form of control which the student exercises over himself, and which keeps him from behaving in a manner that would suggest to faculty or his peers—many of whom are upset— that he is not worried. Students, with few exceptions, did not like to hear that others thought that they were taking examinations lightly: "I didn't want to walk around like some superhuman being that was learning the stuff without suffering for it."

Hostility

As examinations approached and stress increased, students reported a great deal more hostility than before toward the faculty. The hostility allowed the student to relieve some of the building tension. Small injustices loomed large, and what would ordinarily be interpreted as insignificant now was attributed to the "insensitive, callous, faculty." As one student said: "I'm hostile to all the faculty members, even the ones I consider my friends. I even feel hostile towards the ones I'm closest to. It's kind of a generalized hostility to them. Maybe they can understand."

For some students, especially those who have failed on previous attempts, hostility is considerable, even to the point where the student has fantasies of aggressive acts against faculty. Of course, only a small portion of this hostility was expressed, but faculty often note the growing hostility of students as examinations approach.

Often the student will anchor his hostility on actual legitimate complaints that he might have about the examination situation, but the hostility is usually greater than is merited by the complaint.

I think there should be specific feedback on why you rated low or high . . . and you just get generalizations.

I'm kind of disturbed that they are not going to tell us what the schedule of examinations is until we get there on Monday.

These criticisms serve, in other words, as reference points around which the student can organize his feelings of aggression toward the faculty. The latter statement above was made by a few students who used this as a take-off point on which to elaborate how inconsiderate and unfair the faculty were. However, when realistic criticisms were not available, students found other things to complain about:

I'm disturbed they are giving the examinations in the room . . . on the third floor where they have debates. I've never been in it. It's going to take me a while to become comfortable there.

These complaints are manifestations of the extreme tension the students experienced as examinations approached. In general, however, student feelings toward faculty (especially among second-year students) were friendly. Therefore, among this group, blame was usually generalized and externalized: the system being at fault, both students and faculty were trapped in its abuses.

The direct expression of hostility against faculty often created considerable problems for the more expressive student. Feeling anxious and hostile, he would express his hostility openly and then worry about the retaliatory consequences. This made the student feel even more hostile, and, if this reaction were not broken in some way, he might have become seriously angry or depressed.

Seeking Support

As stress increased, the student sought support from other students, friends, wives, faculty, the investigator, and sometimes anyone present. Faculty, wives, and other students were quite liberal in giving support, and some students would identify very strongly with the source of support. One student, for example, became very interested in a subarea of the field because a faculty member who gave him considerable support was interested in this area; by developing this interest, the student was able not only to identify more strongly with the faculty member, but also to request more of his time.

As examinations drew near even isolated students sought support from those around them. Some of the students under considerable stress started talking to almost anyone about examinations; it did not take much to get them talking on the topic. At times they would talk to strangers about their feelings and then feel embarrassed because they had said too much. Interpersonal support, however, continued to be a constant source of reassurance.

Other Defense Techniques

Students utilized a number of other defense techniques. In our discussion, that has been illustrative rather than exhaustive, we have tried to describe the most commonly occurring behaviors, though at various points we have alluded to other less frequent defenses students used.

As we have pointed out, students frequently avoided others who were perceived as likely to arouse anxiety, using banter at times as a means of avoidance. Others attempted to find acceptable possible reasons should they fail: "I would like to know if I would be better in another field." While many verbalized lesser expectations than they themselves had, others sought possible alternatives in case of rejection. But preparing acceptable alternatives—what Hamburg has called the "ace-in-the-hole" defense[8]—while very important in a short-duration stress he studied, was rather unimportant among the student group. Faced with a long-duration stress situation that required considerable involvement and motivation, students could not argue with much force that they had equally adequate alternatives should they fail. Thus, in the student's attempt to control his anxiety, the ace-in-the-hole was not a very effective device.

There were various other ways in which the students defended against anxiety. Many used tranquilizers; some used sleeping pills. Others attempted to externalize responsibility, while some made weak attempts to debunk the goal of passing examinations and their professional or professorial aspirations. What we have tried to emphasize in this chapter is the importance of defense, and some of

8. Unpublished work.

the more common techniques that students used to control their anxiety and facilitate the coping process.

A Dynamic View of
Feelings and Behavior
as Examinations Approach

As the examinations approached and as student anxiety increased, various changes occurred in behavior. Joking increased, and, while students still sought social support and talked a great deal about examinations, they began specifically to avoid certain people who aroused their anxiety. Stomach-aches, asthma, and a general feeling of weariness became common complaints, and other psychosomatic symptoms appeared. The use of tranquilizers and sleeping pills became more frequent.

For those who had started studying intensively at an early date, exhaustion crept in and they lost their desire and motivation to study.

I just don't seem to be picking up things. You know, like I'll look over stuff and I just don't seem to get it. It's very depressing to spend time and not feel it's doing any good. . . . I just wish they would get them over with. It's just bugging me. . . . I'm getting tired of sitting at that desk. I have all sorts of psychosomatic complaints. My back hurts and so forth. . . . I wish they were over. They're so awful. . . . I was about ready to turn myself into [the psychiatric ward] but now I'm taking antidepressant pills.

A number of other students also complained of an inability to concentrate on their studies:

My minute-to-minute motivation seems to have gone down. When I started, I was a real eager beaver but now it seems, the last week or so, I've had a little trouble. If I have a half hour off, I'll sit in the social room rather than study for that half hour.

Lately I've been feeling real depressed. I don't feel that I know anything. I just feel so mentally defective, like what I have done goes into one ear and out the other. . . . Instead of putting in a last-ditch effort, I can't. I'm just sort of tired of the whole business. I'm tired of studying. I'm tired of school. I'm just tired.

While the student feels saturated with study, he still is acutely aware of the short time available for further preparation. Thus he is torn between the feeling that he must study and his inability to concentrate and study effectively, which leads to considerable anxiety, self-doubt, and disgust. As anxiety reaches a high level, students come to agreements not to discuss examinations, but as the saliency of examinations is too great these agreements are rarely maintained. Also, the excessive concern about examinations is reflected in dreams about them. Unreality is another common feeling, the "this isn't happening to me" effect.

As examinations approach, the most common feeling is one of unpreparedness and impending disaster, although these reports of impending doom usually are disqualified in some way. The student, for example, will predict doom and then declare that he must be pretty stupid to say something as silly as that. Listed below are some of the indications students gave that failure was imminent.

I feel now, rather unrealistically, I think, that I can't remember any names. I can't remember this. I can't remember that. I feel unprepared for this.

I spoke to [student C] . . . about how depressed we were. . . . The main thing he hopes is that they'll let him take them again. He keeps saying this over and over because he's now in one of these stages which I think we all go through, where you

just feel that there's no possibility of passing and that you are
a failure.

I kept having the feeling like I'm going to fail and that I
don't know anything.

When the examinations are nearly upon the student,
anxiety is very high, even for those rated as low-anxiety
persons, although students do fluctuate between confidence and anxiety. Since studying is difficult, the student
questions his motivation, interest, and ability in the field.
He reassures himself that he does not care how well he
does—that all he really wants out of the process is the
Ph.D. degree. Even four weeks prior to examinations 82
per cent of the students reported that they had said to
themselves, "All I really want from this process is the
Ph.D. degree." They attempted to defend against their
feelings by behaving in a silly, manic way, and avoidance
joking became very prevalent. Expectation levels were set
lower and lower, and many of the students jokingly talked
about what they were going to do after they failed or how
they were going to prepare for examinations the next time
they took them. It appears that for the student supreme
confidence at this point was considered not only presumptuous, but sacrilegious. Under these conditions the group
became very cohesive and individuals became supportive
of one another and exclusive of younger students in the
department.

In Chapter 8 we shall take a slight detour and attempt
to look at the student in his family setting and see how
this setting was affected by examinations and by how the
student regarded examinations. The student's role involvements with his family were important in his adaptive
attempt, and often the behavior of the family made a
considerable difference in the extent to which the student
experienced "stress."

8

THE FAMILY AND
THE EXAMINATIONS

> [Examinations are] a large monster standing on
> the horizon. . . . That's the way they have been
> for us, standing there. And there's nothing you
> can do about them. [My husband] has been pre-
> paring for them, and everything has to give way
> to this.

OF THE TWENTY-TWO STUDENTS under study thirteen were married, and one was engaged. Eight of the
couples had children, and two others were expecting their
first child. Twelve of thirteen spouses were interviewed a
few weeks prior to examinations regarding the effect of
the examinations on the family. This chapter will be
primarily concerned with some general statements about
the family based on these interviews and those with the
students.

The response of the family to the examination situation is greatly dependent on the organization of the family
before examinations. If the marriage is harmonious, the
family can be cohesive and instrumental in helping the
student to perform at his maximum. However, if the marriage is shaky, the examinations can serve to aggravate and
stimulate further disagreements and conflicts.

The family organization is based on the mutual expectations that the members hold of one another. If the husband's picture of his own role and his performance is consistent with what his wife expects of him, and, if the wife's picture of her role is consistent with the expectations that her husband has of her, family life is likely to be harmonious. As discrepancies in mutual expectations widen, difficulties develop. Expectations are not fully stable, however. As the needs of family life demand flexibility and change, expectations must shift from time to time, depending on the needs of the members in their other social roles outside the family.

In a sense, taking preliminary examinations required such a shift. The student who was taking courses and had other work obligations now had to find sufficient time to study so that he could pass examinations. The expectation of most of the spouses was that the student had the right to be absolved from his usual familial responsibilities—at least for a time—so that he might give his full energies and attention to studying. This of course meant that social and recreational activities for most students diminished. The evenings and weekends spent at the office increased, and the usual attentions the student gave to his family were redirected to examination preparation. Thus the expression "after writtens" became as much a meaningful phrase for the student's spouse as it was for the student, for that phrase generally meant the time when the family would return to normal.

Most of the married students—in fact, all but one—changed their expectations of their spouses to some degree. In every case where I spoke to the spouse these changes in expectations were mutually perceived, and in most cases the spouse cooperated. In the situations where the spouse was not cooperative, difficulties in the family were readily apparent.

The change in expectations usually came about by some mutual agreement that prior to examinations studying would receive great attention; leisure activities would be reduced; and the student would cut down on his responsibilities around the house.

[My husband] spends less and less time at home than he would ordinarily. He gets up early and comes home for about forty-five minutes to an hour for dinner, and that's about all I see of him. And he comes home late at night so that he doesn't have as much time to spend with us at night . . . I'm usually in bed by the time he gets home . . . I think it's worth it; it's necessary. I don't resent it, although there are times I would like to go out but we just can't. . . . We cut out completely our one night a week. Even when we have someone for dinner, it's just for dinner, and then he's gone.

We don't do too many things together. There are a lot of things we would like to do. . . . We just don't feel like we can, because he doesn't have the time, and I don't care for going alone.

A husband of one of the students tells how he assumed more responsibility around the house:

I do take some of the load off. . . . I feel relatively comfortable about it because I'm not that much demanding in the role business, although I will use it at times to avoid doing certain things. But I recognize that it's a real strain, and so I try to do what I can to make things easier.

At times it is the wife who changes her expectations of herself and attempts to convince the husband that she understands the way it should be although he, himself, has not made demands to be absolved of family responsibilities.

When he came in at night, he would play with the [children] while I prepared supper . . . and he usually bathes them. By the time he finishes bathing them, I'm through with supper and we eat and then we both dress them for bed and play with them awhile, and it'll be about seven, seven-thirty. . . . It hasn't changed with [my husband] as much as with me. I feel guilty, I guess, that I'm having him come in and take out a good two and a half hours. . . . He should be able to go ahead and study until I get dinner ready for him. It doesn't seem to bother him half as much as it bothers me in that respect. . . . It's my own expectation [of myself]. I get more upset over it than he does. . . . He says, "It's all right. I can go ahead and help you and study later."

I figure that if he doesn't pass, he doesn't pass. At least he tried. . . . That's all he can do, really. He can't do anything more than try. But, at least, give it a good try . . . I told him that . . . I'd rather have him study than have a good time going out some place.

The family with harmonious relationships as measured by lack of conflict is one where the husband tries not to make new demands, while the wife bends backwards to attempt to fulfill the demands she knows her husband does not want to make. The families with less harmonious relationships are marked by the opposite situation; the husband (student) seems to demand too much, while the wife resists his demands too much. In a sense the family becomes engaged in a "tug-of-war."

Husband: She gets upset when I go to the [building] at night which I have been doing recently. It's just impossible to study at home . . . the baby crying and she wants to talk and play records. She just does not have much sympathy beyond studying eight hours a day, five days a week. She wants me home for lunch and so on. There's consistent pressure.

Wife: Writtens are not that important to me. I guess that's pretty average and universal . . . I take it for granted that he is going to pass. I don't do any worrying about it . . . I don't seem very fully involved in this. I wonder if other wives are the same way or if it's because of other things that I'm not completely wrapped up in this.

The wife's perception was interesting in light of the husband's position in the communication structure. Like the husband, the wife sought some basis for social comparison. This particular wife was isolated (as was her husband) and had no way of evaluating her attitudes and feelings about the examinations against those held by other wives. This lack of social comparison left her uncertain as to how she should feel about the demands being made upon her by her husband. Another couple had similar problems:

Husband: She gets kind of depressed about my working all the time and never going out. We've had several violent clashes over this. . . . I generally stay out much later, so she goes to bed before I do. This kind of bothers her also.

Wife: Family life has gone completely down the drain. There is none. [My husband] has become a creature behind the book. . . . As far as major responsibilities go, especially timing elements, if he has to go somewhere on time, it doesn't matter who else in the family has to be where. . . . The baby cries for his ten o'clock bottle; [my husband] hits the ceiling, "He's been crying all night." Of course, this isn't true, but it may seem that way to him. Or I ask him to do something off the top of my head; instead of saying, "No, I'm busy," he may get angry because I'm imposing on his time. . . . You enter marriage with the idea that it's a 50-50 proposition with regard to some things. You expect to see the other partner at least part of the time and have him take a little bit of the load. . . . But suddenly he tells you, "I wouldn't be here on week-ends; I wouldn't be here so and so; I can't do this, that, and the other." This comes as rather a shock. "I can't go to the store; I can't help you with the dishes; I can't baby-sit with the baby; you can't expect me to do anything." It's quite a shock.

She indicated that her husband made other demands as well as the demand that he be absolved from familial responsibility:

I have to make sure that there is always a particular type of tobacco there at a particular time. These are small things, but they are irritating . . . or that there are sharpened pencils in the house. And, also, larger accommodations: willing to give up something I want to do to go to the library to get a book or something else.

The tug-of-war here is apparent. Both members of the pair demanded too much and both were willing to give in too little.

There seems little doubt that the family is subjected to considerable stress during the examination period and, to some extent, during graduate school, especially if the partner is not a student also or does not have some interests of her own to pursue. The couples who made the easiest adaptation to the examination situation were those without children, where both were students, or where the student's spouse had a job she liked. The quality of the relationship of the student to his spouse could affect whether or not the family made a smooth adaptation to the examination situation or whether conflict was to develop. As some of the wives recognized, the examinations did present a situation that could easily provide a conflict if the family were so inclined.

Everyone's raw edges seem to be sticking out more often. . . . When you are living under constant tension you expect this, so piddling things that wouldn't ordinarily bother anyone in the family are of utmost importance.

I think [my spouse's] going to school complements my going to school, and it's helpful because it gives us common ground, so to speak. If I was studying at night and [my spouse] had nothing to do, it would be an unbalanced situation.

Families had two general reactions toward examinations. They either became more cohesive and mobilized together against the external challenge, or the challenge itself threatened the family. In many ways the examinations presented a situation that could lead to better understanding and more empathy within the family, but, when the relationship was shaky between husband and wife, examinations also could lead to bickering and conflict. A common complaint of the wives, for example, was loneliness. This was especially true of those wives who had children and whose husbands studied at the office. Since the wife was tied to the home, because of the children, this limited her mobility and added to her loneliness.

I don't see him as much as I would like to, naturally. Our social life is cut down considerably. . . . Occasionally, I get sort of irritated, but most of the time, I think, I'm fairly reasonable about it. . . . There's no point in arguing about it. Then he gets upset and can't study. . . . If I really get lonely—if I don't see somebody—I go berserk, and I either go to talk to a neighbor across the street or I talk to [my husband] and he says, "Maybe we can spend a couple of hours and go to the movies tonight."

Wives' Involvement in the Examination Process

The families that readily adapted to the stress of examinations, that is, who did not argue about changes in family life due to examinations, were those where the couples unified and mobilized together to deal with the challenge. It is particularly interesting that in general wives were not well informed about examinations in an objective sense. In the families that adapted readily, spouses were extremely supportive and accepted the student's definition of the situation, whatever that might be. Thus the spouse seemed to enter the defense system of the student and support it. Spouses within the families that adapted well to the examination process had much the same attitude toward the examinations—rationalizations and all—as did their partners. Possible failure was perceived not as an attribute of the partner but, rather, as a reflection of the abuses of the system. On the other hand, in the families that had more difficulties in adaptation, the spouse seemed to remain outside the partner's definition of the situation and viewed the examinations more objectively than the student was willing to do. Below are some examples to illustrate this point:

If he doesn't pass, it's not because he doesn't know the material and isn't able, but simply because he can't get it down at the time wanted in sufficient quantity. . . . He doesn't feel it's necessary to write just to have volume. He wants to say something when he writes.

I think [my husband] has the ability. And I would think that he just messed up. On another given day he would have done all right. Something just was bothering him.

One wife whose husband had failed on a prior attempt reported:

To me it's rather a ridiculous situation since I know how he studied to begin with. It's hard for me to understand how he failed and especially considering his past record. . . . Right at the point that he needed reinforcement he didn't get it.

. . . For some people, possibly, failing would give them motivation, but for him it was definitely a very bad setback . . . I think [failing him] was unjust. I heard all these stories that they were toughening their policies. Perhaps this was it. He happened to be one of the unfortunate ones who didn't have someone to stay with him to say that he isn't going to be one of the ones; and possibly he didn't do well under the strain he was under at the time. . . . I wouldn't see [failure] as any reflection of his abilities at all, because I know of what he can do and I know what he's capable of doing. . . . I feel there's something wrong with the testing system if he fails again. In fact, I thought that the first time.

If the wife views the husband and the examination process objectively, difficulties are likely to evolve because the student is defending, and defense to maintain itself requires interpersonal support. The following quotes are taken from a discussion with a wife of one of the students who did not view the examinations through the eyes of her husband and who was not as supporting as many of the other wives. The transcript starts after she has just told the questioner *(Q)* that she took it for granted that her husband would pass the examinations.

Q: Is he sure?
Wife: I don't think he thinks about it really. I'm pretty confident he doesn't think about it. He couldn't. My goodness, if he sat there thinking about it, he'd never get any studying done.
Q: As a matter of fact, some people do sit and, instead of reading, worry about passing the examinations.
Wife: Well, it's understandable, but it's unfortunate.
Q: Well, some people can't help it.
Wife: True. Well, it helps if you talk about it to someone.
Q: How would you feel about him if he failed?
Wife: I don't know. I don't know whether I would think of him as a failure or if I would be more tolerant. Hopefully, I

would be understanding and tolerant rather than say, "Look what you've done. You ruined my life." I would at least try to be understanding because it would be a much greater blow to him than it would ever be to me. He's personally involved. . . . I may cut myself off from him.

Children

Often there was some tendency for children to be affected by the examination situation, although this seemed to be primarily a redefinition of when "daddy" was available.

He has always helped so much with [the children] from the very first day. When he came home, we spent an awful lot of time together. And, before, I would just come in, "Would you come and help me with this or that?" And now I feel that I shouldn't do that. . . . He [studies] in the bedroom. [The children] go knock on the door, "Is daddy gone?" They know that when he goes in there, he's gone, and they know that even if they holler "daddy," he's not supposed to come in and play with them. He would. He used to be more prone to. If they knocked on the door, he would come out and play with them a little while. Now he doesn't and they realize that. . . . I tell them, "Daddy is studying; come on, and leave daddy alone," and they say, "Daddy is studying, daddy is studying."

[Our child would say]: "I want to go out and do something," say for a ride or a hike in the woods; and I would say, "Well, daddy can't do that today because he has some tests coming up and he has to study for it so he can pass the tests. . . ."

The tension and anxiety that the family feels about the examinations also may affect the children, but we have no data relevant to this. The only major change we discovered was a redefinition of roles relative to the child, although even this did not always occur.

Plans for the Future

It is obvious that the outcome on the examinations will determine in large part the family's future plans—where they will go, what they will do, and how much money they will have. The family is very much involved in the consequences of examinations and the spouse gives considerable thought to them. Future plans that could be made are weighed in relation to examinations.

I went to [X college] my first two years . . . and I have jokingly at various times since we were married said, "You should teach at [X college] some time." It's quite interesting . . . there was a job offer from [X college] for someone with a Master's, and we toyed very seriously with the idea of applying for the job and finally decided not to. We didn't want to give the faculty any legitimate excuse for dismissing him with a good conscience if such were imminent.

Failure on the examinations often meant that many plans "went down the drain." One wife, whose husband had failed the examinations on a prior attempt, described the process:

It was a big disappointment. We planned being out of here and gone by this time. We already had our plans made and everything. . . . We made plans to make an extended trip. I was going to quit work and, after he failed the writtens, he decided he'd go ahead and leave. And that was the plan. . . . I went ahead and quit. After I quit, he decided to stay this year. . . . He decided about two days before we were ready to leave. So then I had to look for [another job]. It's been nothing but a waste of time this last year and a half . . . and, of course, finances enter into it.

Another wife described how the family's planning is contingent on the writtens:

We talked about what we would do to prepare ourselves, and
we tried to look at it sensibly. We are both affected more
deeply than we want to show on the surface. . . . [my husband]
came home from school one day and said, "The writtens
come up in April, and I think we should both be preparing
for the possibility that I might fail them. We should be making some plans about what we might do and so forth."

"After examinations" represents to the families the
resumption both of the usual patterns of family life and
of old roles relative to spouse, children, and friends. As
the following statements indicate, plans and activities are
put off until after examinations.

We both have shelved [talking about taking a trip]. We
haven't at all discussed it at this point, feeling that this is
just something that'll have to wait.

You know how long it's going to be; and with me it's just
sort of, well, if you can hang on for three more weeks, two
more weeks, one more week, it'll be over.

Constantly someone was dropping in. That was a problem
for a while. . . . They just drop by . . . and they were constantly doing that. And, finally, I just had to tell some of the
wives that [my husband] is studying more now.

The housework is left undone and such things of this nature.
. . . [My wife] feels she owes it to the writtens.

[I tell friends], "We'll get together with you when writtens
are over because [my fiancé] is studying and we don't do
much." [My fiancé] and I are planning to do lots of things
when writtens are over. We don't do a lot of things because
he studies so often. . . . I look forward to these things when
they are over so we can do thus and so.

Although having a family does make the examination
a more important event, the family also may serve to
support the student who is taking them. The spouse

usually serves as a sympathetic outlet for the expression of anxiety and depression.

Since I'm in much closer contact with my wife . . . I spend much more time with her than I do with the students. She is there at the moment of mood changes, so that when I feel very downhearted about my prospects I let her know about this and she, of course, encourages me, and says, "That's silly, you know you are just as bright as anyone else," or "you got better marks all along so you can pass the writtens," and things to that effect. And then I tell her when I'm jubilant and bowling with joy, "I'll rack up" and things like that, and she says, "Of course you are."

The student taking examinations wants more than simple affirmation of confidence from his spouse. He also wants involvement from the spouse and an expression of concern. In our study, most wives did get involved in the examinations and experienced anxiety and upset as did their husbands. This made the family deprivation seem smaller because it was not only the student who was attempting to pass examinations, but the family as well. In the families where the wife did not become involved, supportive moves were ineffective since the student wanted the spouse to accept his doubts as well as his hopes.

Q: Do you discuss your examinations and how you feel about them with [your wife]?

Student: I've tried to sometimes with her and she said, "I have complete confidence in you."

Q: How do you feel about that? Do you think she understands your examination situation very realistically?

Student: I don't think so. . . . She couldn't understand what the tensions are. . . . I've tried [to communicate this to her], but this goes over like a lead balloon.

In the above example the wife affirmed her confidence in her husband but did not indicate real understanding of the experience her husband was having. In the more harmonious families the spouse plays a different role vis-à-vis the student.

I try not to let him know if they upset me. I say, "You'll do all right." . . . It was about two weeks ago, he had this big examination and . . . since then he hasn't gotten down to work as well as he was doing before . . . I got upset. And he tried to calm me down. He said, "I'll try to study even though I won't pass the examination . . . I'll have to try my hardest."

In general, spouses do not provide blind support. They perceive the kinds of support the student wants and then they provide it. The wife who becomes worried about examinations also may provide more support than the spouse who says, "I'm not worried. You will surely pass." Indeed, since there is a chance that the student will not pass, the person who is supportive in a meaningful sense will not give blind assurance. Rather, she will seek to find the realistic limits of the situation, the weaknesses of the spouse, and the anxieties and tensions that are being experienced; and then she will attempt to help reduce these. Often a statement to the effect—"Do the best you can"— is more supportive than—"I'm sure you are going to do well." The latter statement adds to the student's burden, for not only must he fear the disappointment of not passing, but also the loss of respect in the eyes of his spouse.

Most wives, however, were supportive in a significant way. Only four of the thirteen students reported that their partners were not fully supportive. Yet there still were complaints. Students were asked how often their partners complained about a number of items. According to student reports, all of the thirteen spouses at one time or another had made some complaints about not having enough money. Six of the thirteen spouses complained about this either very or fairly often. Eleven of the thirteen spouses had complained about not being able to go out enough, but only five of the thirteen complained about this either very or fairly often. Nine of the thirteen spouses complained that the student was not doing enough around the house, but only four of these complained about this very or fairly often. Eight of the thirteen spouses complained about the students not being home enough; five of them complained about this very or fairly often.

Thus family life around examination time is not devoid of complaints. And, in some ways the adaptation required of the spouse is as difficult as that expected of the student.

9

THE EXAMINATIONS:
BEFORE AND AFTER

THE FIRST of the written examinations was scheduled for Monday morning at nine o'clock. At eight-fifteen the researcher arrived and found a comfortable position in the department lounge. As nine o'clock approached, students appeared seemingly tense and earnest. One student came into the lounge and wrote a set of "Written Rationalizations" on the board that evoked a few smiles. Most students glanced into the lounge as they appeared and then went off. Some gathered in the lounge; one studying flash cards, another casually turning the pages of a *Life* magazine, a third just sitting twiddling his thumbs. Across the hall, four students gathered in one of the offices and their loud bantering could be heard. Others paced the hall, waiting to be given their examination, and anxious to get to work. The researcher who had developed a fairly good relationship with most of the group had a left-out feeling. The locus of interaction moved away from wherever he happened to be at any moment. He could hear the bantering going on across the hall, but when he appeared it stopped. In one of the later interviews one of the four students described the situation in this way: "We didn't want to talk to you. You were the reality; the truth. We were all going around hypermanicky, denying. . . . I was trying to forget the whole thing."

Let us move back a few days and attempt to describe the dynamics of behavior just prior to the examinations. Although many students had their unreality feelings broken by the need to make a last-ditch effort to study intensively, some still had the feeling that "this can't be happening to me." The exhaustion that had developed earlier seemed to wear off as students began their final cramming sessions for the examinations. The pattern of work was irregular; all of the students experienced some ups and downs, but the over-all intensity of study was high.

The weekend prior to examinations, severe psychosomatic symptoms seemed to appear. A few students actually became sick, probably attributable in part to the increased vulnerability resulting from the physical and mental exhaustion that had accompanied study and from keeping late hours. Many students reported having stomach-aches, anxiety attacks, increased problems with asthma, and some rashes and allergies. Appetite and eating patterns also seemed affected, and a number of students reported difficulty in sleeping. On the morning of examinations most students reported stomach pains; a number reported diarrhea; and a few reported that they had been unable to hold their breakfast. As one student said: "I was real scared. I never was so scared in my life.

Like, what am I going to do? I just won't be able to do it. . . . I felt that I was going to fall apart." Most students reported considerable relief of anxiety once they got started on the first examination. The stomach difficulties subsided, and they were able to direct their attention and energies to the task at hand. One student explained: "Taking it is not as bad as anticipating it. It's not nearly so bad. . . . You don't have time to worry while you are doing it."

During the examination week the student's feeling states are highly dependent on how he perceives he did on the examinations he has already taken. If he believes that he is doing satisfactorily, he begins to feel more comfortable and confident. If he perceives that he is doing badly, he is upset and his ruminating interferes somewhat with his performance on subsequent examinations, at least in his own mind. The student in working on the examinations gets some feeling as to how things are going. After each examination students congregated and discussed the questions to some extent, as well as the answers they had given. Through such discussion the student got an opportunity to make an appraisal of his performance relative to the others. The student who already had perceived that he had done a poor job attempted to avoid this discussion; those who felt that they had done well hashed over their answers and gave each other encouragement and support.

During this period the student group became very cohesive and excluded outsiders in a way similar to their treatment of the researcher. A number of students commented on the in-group atmosphere that developed during the week of examinations:

It seems as if the people are much closer . . . during the

examinations. . . . There was a great deal of support during [them]. . . . It seemed that during the examinations, the people taking them had very little to do with anyone who wasn't. Some of the first-year students made comments about how are you doing, and people would just say "all right" and leave. Everyone spent their time with the other people who were taking examinations, or we would all congregate in the social room before them and joke about them. . . . It seems that during the time you're taking them, you are sort of wrapped up in them, and it's much more frightening to think of someone else or yourself failing them. Then you can empathize better with people who felt they weren't doing very well. . . . There was just a lot of tension built up during the examinations. And then there was just a big release, joking, laughing. It's also that you have a common base of things to talk about. . . . You sort of had the feeling that [people not taking the examinations] couldn't understand how it was, taking them.

The group was very in-groupish so that nobody else could really talk with us or anything. We just talked among ourselves. . . . As long as we stayed together and didn't talk to outside people we were all okay because we were in the same boat. . . . I guess we were pretty friendly toward each other, but hostile toward other people.

As the examination week progressed, students continued to devote their main energies to the examinations. The main interfering stimuli were cognitions that there were important things they knew but had forgotten that they should have used in answering this and that question. Also, in comparing their answers with those given by others, they were made anxious by the inevitable discrepancies that were noted. The students who felt that all was going well behaved in a considerably different way from those less sure, and these differences were detected by other students.

There were times when a person who did very well on a particular area would be in very good spirits, and others wouldn't be and they would just disappear.

On the Friday of examination week most of the students were exhausted, and examinations were followed by a period of relaxation: fishing, beach trips, and the like. While there was a feeling of some relief over completing examinations, few students felt certain that they had passed. All of them reported that there had been questions on which they had performed poorly; as time progressed, students could think of better answers they might have written, discover mistakes they had made, or come to the conclusion that other students had approached the questions in a more effective fashion than they. These feelings led to considerable anxiety and uncertainty.

As the waiting period before they heard the results began, most students were too tired to worry much about them. But with increased time, contact with others, and discussion about examinations, doubts increased. No one felt presumptuous enough to "bait the gods" by contending openly that he had surely passed, and some became convinced that they in fact had not passed and were talking about plans for another concerted effort to pass examinations the next time around. Those who felt sure that they had done poorly began to develop anticipatory failure reactions. As the week progressed and it was known that faculty members were reading the papers, students became very sensitive to cues. In fact, the sensitivity to faculty behavior became so great that some students decided to avoid going to the building so as not to become aroused.

Some of the after-examination reactions were significant enough to merit more detailed discussion. Let us start by letting one of the anxious students describe how he felt during the week. While somewhat more intense

than the average student, in substance this description is
in part typical of student reaction:

When examinations were over, I felt pretty much drained . . .
[I had] sort of a lost feeling. I couldn't sit down, I couldn't
work, I couldn't study. I didn't really feel that I could do
much of anything. I goofed off a lot. . . . In the interim
period, I was fairly convinced that I had failed. . . . I was
convinced that I wouldn't take them over again. I just didn't
want to go through that experience. I wasn't sure what I was
going to do. . . . As time went on, my doubts began to increase more and more. I sort of had time to think about the
answers I had given. I had come across various things in
studying and so forth that I was doing after examinations
that clearly showed mistakes that I made as I took them. As
time went on, I became more and more pessimistic. I was
quite sure that I hadn't passed.

Cue Processes

During examinations many students perceive that faculty members become aloof and distant, that they become
impersonal toward those taking examinations. The reports differ. While some students reported perceiving the
faculty as cooler and more aloof, others rejected this
opinion. At any rate the students themselves became aloof
and in-groupish in some sense and expressed considerable
hostility indirectly toward faculty. When examinations
end and faculty begin grading, students become extremely
sensitive to the expressions and behavior of the faculty.
They interpret faculty behavior as meaningful in regard
to their examination performance.

I've not discussed it much with anyone. . . . [Professor X]
asked me how I did. In asking me, it sounded as if he had
some information [that] I did pretty well. The way he asked
it wasn't a question. . . . This week we were talking about

jobs and things. . . . If we weren't going to pass, they wouldn't have discussed this. Usually, they'll be aloof.

I was just leaving the building and [Professor Y] is a grader. And I don't know [Professor Y] from Adam and he impresses me as being a stern authoritarian guy. I don't even know him. He just looks that way. . . . I walked in this morning to the office, and he turned around and looked at me and smiled and said hello. This is the first time he ever did this so that I can read into it that he read my paper and he liked it, and he knows who I am indirectly.

The feedback I've had has been very encouraging . . . just the casual greetings with faculty members. . . . If one were going to fail, I think that the faculty members might be a little aloof, for they are sort of preparing the student for a great disappointment. I think that if they expected him to pass, they probably would show some encouragement and enthusiasm. This has been my experience since the examinations have been over; the fact that various faculty members I have seen have all been very optimistic and pleasant.

Cues, however, were not always perceived favorably, and, when they were not, they were a source of considerable anxiety. One student described the cues he perceived during examination week that were quite different from those he perceived after examinations:

[Professor B] hardly spoke to me although we passed each other in the hall many times. It's a little bit odd since he's my advisor and since he's almost always very friendly . . . and [Professor E] . . . I saw he never initiated greetings and on one occasion he walked way around me as if he was trying to keep me from seeing him. . . . It seemed to fit in with his other behavior because I would occasionally be standing right beside him, say, in the office by the desk, and he didn't speak. At least once or twice I spoke to him and he just grunted.

Others perceived impending doom:

I would pick up little paranoid bits of data here and there. I guess I was pretty upset about my statistics and I was doing some statistics for [Doctor *F*] and we came across a problem. And he said, "You work on this and see what you can do with it and, if you come up with a solution, I'll add two points to your statistics grade." Immediately, I started ruminating. What does he know about my statistics? Do I really need two points? So I actually confronted him with these feelings later and he said it actually was just a figure of speech and that he hadn't heard anything.

A number of students recognized that cues are hazardous criteria on which to base opinions and that autistic perception does operate.

[Professor *F*] said, "How are you?" and I said, "fine." He said he was glad someone had a realistic outlook . . . I said, "hmmm" . . . then I said, "No, I shouldn't go around thinking that people mean these deep significant things."

I'm not going to fall for that stuff because I saw [Professor *H's* wife] this morning . . . and she smiled at me and said, "Hi," and looked at me a long time. She always does that anyway. . . . Well, I could feel the wheels going around. I'm really going to be bad about that.

When I wasn't working, I just stood away. I realized that the more I would stay there, the more paranoid I would become. I sort of detected it already. A guy would say "hello" and so forth. I realized that this was just bad, so I stood away.

The perception of cues is keen and at times students do successfully denote changes toward them in faculty attitudes. For example, a week prior to the announcement of final results the researcher overheard a faculty discussion to the effect that one of the students had, from all indications, performed quite poorly on the questions read thus far, and that, from the way it looked, he would fail. Not only did this student report a change in attitude toward him by some of the faculty members, but other students around him also noticed this. The student under discussion, still desiring to retain hope of a favorable outcome, attempted to find an explanation for this change in attitude he thought he perceived:

I kind of have the feeling that [Professor Z] was avoiding me. This may not be because of examinations but because I was pretty short with him as I was coming back after the [L] area examination. As I said, I was feeling pretty low. He asked me how I did. I gave him a pretty short reply. It may well be that he was reacting to this and not to the larger situation. I don't know how to take this. I'm trying to hold off making an irrevocable decision.

Other students around this student had a more certain picture of what this meant:

It appears that he will probably not pass. . . . Mainly they do not talk to him. They keep away from him. He went into [Doctor N's] office. [Doctor N] acted as if he didn't have time to talk. In other words, he wants to terminate the thing pretty quickly.

[Student C] is really quite worried about the outcome of the examinations. He's afraid from these same kind of personal cues . . . that there is a good possibility of his failing. He works very closely with [Professors N and Z] and the relationship has always been quite friendly and relaxed. But he's noticed that it's become sort of less and less friendly. And now he senses when he goes into [Professor N's] office, the attitude he experiences is that [Professor N] would like him to get out as quickly as possible. . . . He also is experiencing a similar aloofness or unfriendliness on the part of [Professor Z]. So he interprets this as an indication that he may be up for failure.

The students who best perceive cues appeared to be those who reported these cues being emitted by faculty members with whom they had had stable relationships over some period of time. If they knew the faculty mem-

ber fairly well, the detected change they had noted in behavior could in fact be significant. In situations where
they knew faculty members only casually, real bases for
evaluating such change were less likely. In the latter case
students perceived cues that were mostly favorable.
These served as a mode of relieving anxiety and uncertainty about the outcome; in other words, they represented autistically perceived phenomena.

During the student discussions of answers during examination week students, as we have already pointed out,
were sensitive to how their peers seemed to be doing.
Students who themselves had done poorly left the group
rather quickly. Those who participated in the discussions
obtained gratification from being able to compare their
answers favorably with those of other students. One student, especially, allowed others to use him for favorable
social comparisons by stressing the idiosyncratic answers
he had written on examinations. On one occasion he told
other students that he had responded to an identification
item with, "What is this, an anagram game?" The flippant
answers he reported made others assume that he would
surely fail the examinations, when, in fact, he had done
well. The statement that follows was typical of student
reaction to his comments:

I guess I thought that [student *P*] didn't have any chance at
all. . . . He seems to have been in some kind of schizoid state
most of the year. Rumors were going back and forth during
the examinations that he was writing garbage and porno-
graphic material on the examinations; that he wasn't really
answering the questions. He seemed to take a fairly flippant
attitude toward the examinations, coming in late and leaving
early.

Interestingly the cues used by students to support their

contention that the student under discussion was not writing intelligent answers to questions were based primarily on the fact that this student outwardly did not seem to take the examinations seriously and did not seem to reflect the respectful awe shared by the others. This, of course, was annoying information to assimilate and students used this as evidence that the student must be writing "garbage" on examinations. In a sense the student encouraged such a definition by eliciting ambiguous information about the kinds of responses he was making on the examinations. Also, during a few examinations this student left early because he found them rather easy, and felt that he was able to answer the questions satisfactorily in less than the assigned time; his departure was interpreted by others, who would not consider leaving the examinations early, as further evidence of the likely incompetence of his answers. The finding here, in some respects, is similar to a finding by Schachter and Burdick[1] in a study of rumor transmission concerning a child who was unexpectedly called out of class by the principal of a school: children who liked the student developed rumors attributing some favorable outcomes to the situation; children who did not, attributed an unfavorable outcome. In the situation among our students the behavior and lack of concern of the student under question could have been interpreted either way; the students chose to interpret it unfavorably.

Students who did poorly on some questions would feel relieved if they learned that other students also had had difficulty with the same questions. In addition, gratification and relief came from the information that professors

---

1. S. Schachter and H. A. Burdick, "A Field Experiment on Rumor Transmission and Distortion," *J. Abnorm. Soc. Psychol., 50,* 1955, 363-371.

could not identify all of the identification items on the examinations. As one of the students put it, "If our gold will rust, what will our iron do?"

Most of the defensive devices already mentioned in an earlier chapter also were utilized at this time. Students sought comforting cognitions and favorable comparisons as well as other evidence that they would pass. This period, however, was different in that students now found themselves unable to keep busy, and their restlessness increased their anxiety.

The anxiety over the results increased to its most intense point during the day of the final faculty meeting, especially during the hours of the meeting in the late afternoon. As tension and anxiety mounted, students found themselves incapacitated for work.

Yesterday, it got to be too much, sort of. I did get very anxious during the afternoon, especially. I don't know. I had sort of the feeling that I had kept on this long—I had kept myself from feeling very anxious—and it was getting right down to the wire and I just couldn't hold on any more. . . . I just felt very nervous and very anxious to hear. I was shaking and in generally pretty bad shape. . . . As yesterday evening approached, I kept thinking more and more [so] that the bad [answers] got bigger in my mind. They grew in importance and I was focusing on them and ruminating about how poorly I had done on some questions and so on.

While this student's feelings were very intense, all of the students reported similar heightening of anxieties as decision time came. Some loitered around Central Building waiting for the faculty meeting to end; others avoided the building, hoping to keep anxiety at a minimum. During this time the faculty was meeting to evaluate the results.

The Faculty Meeting

A day prior to the meeting, a faculty examination committee met and compiled the student scores on the various examinations. Each examination had been read independently by two graders. After reading an area the grader would score it as either strong Ph.D., Ph.D. pass, M. A. pass, or fail. In addition to each of these scores the faculty member could indicate whether the student had made this level with a very good, average, or minimal performance. Thus, theoretically twelve possible distinctions could be drawn in grading an area. Faculty grading examinations also were asked to indicate qualitative descriptions of the student's performance in the area graded. The examination committee then drew up a result sheet to show the scores of each student in each area, ranking the students in terms of over-all performance. These result sheets were duplicated and distributed to faculty members before the faculty meeting.

At the faculty meeting the results were put on the board and explained, although faculty had already received result sheets. The chairman of the examination committee then announced the examination committee's recommended cutting points. The top ten students were passed unanimously as a group with almost no discussion. The faculty then discussed the students who had performed very poorly, concentrating on the reasons why these students had done as poorly as they did, their performance in the past, and so on. Since these students clearly had failed the examinations, the discussion was more concerned with the kinds of recommendations to be made to them rather than whether they should pass or fail; that is, should they be encouraged to continue, to leave the program, or what?

During the meeting the main discussion was concerned primarily with students who performed marginally; these students were considered both as a group and individually. The discussion covered to some extent their past work, their strengths, their weaknesses, and the like. Questions were raised as to the utility of having these students take the examinations again and as to the effect of anxiety on their performance. After considerable discussion it was agreed to pass these students with the stipulation that they make up certain deficiencies, but with no necessity of repeating the examinations.

Since more detailed consideration of this meeting would involve violating its anonymity and would concern specific criteria taken into account for specific persons, and since this information is peripheral to the main argument of the book, further elaboration will not be necessary. The researcher should point out, however, that in his opinion the meeting was basically objective. In his opinion, also, irrelevant criteria were not used in making decisions. Decisions generally were predetermined by the distribution of scores. Main concern was given to the procedure for establishing cutting points and to the criteria to be used in establishing these cutting points.

What was particularly relevant to the study in respect to the faculty meeting was the form of interaction that took place, since the students had very definite ideas about who would and would not be instrumental in making decisions. Interaction seemed to be dependent on faculty status. While assistant professors often participated, tenure professors not only spoke considerably more but also made more direct statements than did lower-ranking faculty. When assistant professors did participate, they were more likely to make informational and procedural statements that were often neutral in tone. Tenure professors more freely offered their favorable and unfavorable impressions and evaluations.

Twenty-two faculty members participated in the meeting, and, since individuals often spoke simultaneously, it was difficult to keep accurate counts on interaction. Interaction was charted by the observer and one of the younger professors so that some reliability estimate could be made of the observer's count. Reliability was poor, however, especially as a result of the fact that the observer emerged with considerably more remarks than did the other rater. Unfortunately, the second rater stopped rating at points when the discussion became interesting. However, the data of both raters did show similar tendencies.

Although the ratings were considerably different, the ratings of both observers showed that tenure members of the faculty contributed more discussion and more opinionated statements than did the assistant professors.

Table 33—Interaction at the Faculty Meeting

Direct Remarks about Students (Positive and Negative)	Mean Number	Neutral Remarks about Students	Mean Number
Ratings by Observer 1		Ratings by Observer 1	
Tenure professors (N-7)	7.4	Tenure professors (N-7)	3.0
Assistant professors (N-15)*	1.9	Assistant professors (N-15)	1.1
Ratings by Observer 2		Ratings by Observer 2	
Tenure professors (N-7)	5.0	Tenure professors (N-7)	1.3
Assistant professors (N-15)	1.9	Assistant professors (N-15)	.9

*Some nonteaching staff were present at the meeting, while some teaching staff were absent.

When an assistant professor did make pointed remarks, they were usually in regard to the one student with whom he had worked most closely.

A third kind of interaction not charted concerned general comments about the examinations, information irrelevant to student evaluation and procedural comments. The greatest number of such comments was made by the chairman of the department and the chairman of the examination committee. In general, however, it seemed that assistant professors were much more free in participating in these discussions than in those concerned with making a decision about students.

The student predictions of the instrumentality of faculty members in making decisions were not supported by observation of the faculty meeting. In general, the role of assistant professors was not very great in the decision-making process.

A few weeks prior to examinations faculty were asked to indicate how likely each of a number of criteria was to be considered, explicitly or implicitly, in the evaluation and decision regarding a student who had performed marginally on the examinations. The percentage of professors who reported each of the crtieria as either very or fairly likely to be considered in making a final evaluation of the student is presented in Table 34. Students also were asked the same question four weeks after examinations. Their responses are also indicated.

Although all factors are likely to receive at least some attention from faculty members, it is evident from Table 34 that two criteria were most considered—those related to proficiency in past work and those related to ability to contribute to the profession. In many ways the student responses obtained four weeks following examinations were similar to the faculty responses, although there were a few apparent discrepancies. For example, while 68 per cent of the students reported that the effort the student has put in was likely to be considered, only 33 per cent of the faculty members reported this as a factor. Faculty members were much more likely than students to report

Table 34—Percentage of Professors and Students Indicating That It Is Either Very or Fairly Likely That Criteria Will Be Considered for Marginal Students

Criteria	PER CENT OF	
	Faculty (N-21—22)*	Students (N-19)
General ability	100	100
Past grades in courses	86	84
Progress on dissertation research	71	42
Whether he has wife and children	14	6
How much time he has invested	50	42
How much effort he seems to have put in	33	68
His ability to handle technical-experimental problems	86	79
Ability as a (practitioner)	86	47
Teaching ability	52	29
His ability to get along with others	23	32
External disturbing factors likely to have influenced his examination performance	82	58
Personality stability	41	47
Potential for a creative contribution to the field	95	74
Articles, papers, or other contributions to (the field)	82	74

*In some cases twenty-two responses were available, in other cases only twenty-one.

that the student's practical skills were likely to be considered. While 86 per cent of the faculty believed this to be considered, only 47 per cent of the students reported this likely.

Since student response was elicited after the examinations, it is possible that the experience and the reduction of defense needs had changed their perceptions from what they might have been had we asked them about these factors prior to examinations. Therefore it is not clear as to what significance should be attributed to these results. At any rate the results do suggest that when faculty consider nonexamination factors in marginal cases, they choose criteria that relate to professional abilities and potential rather than personal criteria relating to likeability, family needs, and effort.

Factors Associated with Performance

In a book devoted to a study of examinations it is not superfluous to give at least some indications of factors relevant to the study that are associated with performance, even though the variables affecting performance are vastly complicated and can receive but a superficial treatment in our discussion.

There is good reason to believe that performance on examinations can be predicted on the basis of prior information. No doubt, intelligence and preparation are significant factors. Prior to examinations students were asked to indicate those students who they expected would

Table 35—Predictions of Student Performance and Actual Student Performance

Student Performance	PREDICTIONS OF STUDENT PERFORMANCE (By Investigator)			
	High (N=4)	Moderate High (N=4)	Moderate Low (N=5)	Low (N=8)
Top 10 students	4	1	3	2
Bottom 11 students	0	3	2	6

Table 36—Predictions of Student Performance and Actual Performance at Extremes

Student Performance	Predictions by Investigator
Top six students	
1	High
2	High
3	High
4	Moderate low
5	Moderate high
6	High
Bottom six students	
21	Low
20	Moderate low
19	Low
18	Low
17	Low
16	Low

do well on the examinations, and faculty members were asked to indicate those students they felt most likely to be successful professionals. The investigator also made his own ratings based on his own impressions of student adequacy, but largely dependent on the ratings given by students and faculty. The predictions shown in Table 35 do not tell the complete story since the predictions, like the examinations, were very effective in differentiating students at the extremes but very poor within the middle range.

Only one estimate of the twelve extreme cases in Table 36 was very inaccurate. In general, it appears to this investigator that the examinations did not provide information that could not have been obtained in some other fashion. If such examinations are to be justified, it appears that such justification must rest on factors other than their utility for evaluation.

Since student status, position in the communication structure, and anxiety have been major variables in the study, let us now note the extent to which these variables played a role or were related to performance.

Although older students seemed to do more poorly

Table 37—Performance on Examinations and Position in the Communication Structure

Performance on Examinations	POSITION IN THE COMMUNICATION STRUCTURE	
	Three or More Communication Links	Less than Three Communication Links
Top 10 students	2	8
Bottom 11 students	6	5

Table 38—Performance on Examinations and Level of Anxiety

Performance Level	LEVEL OF ANXIETY		
	High	Moderate	Low
Top 10 students	2	4	4
Bottom 11 students	5	3	3

than second-year students on the examinations, there was no difference in the number of older students within the top ten and bottom eleven. Some of the poorest performances, however, did come from older students.

As the data in Tables 37 and 38 show, students more central in the communication structure were more likely to do poorly. Examination of Table 38 also shows that anxiety did seem somewhat related to performance, although it is difficult to differentiate the effects of centrality and anxiety since we showed earlier that centrally located students were more anxious than those peripherally located. Whether students who were anxious and insecure did communicate more about examinations, or whether communication did interfere with performance cannot be answered by the data available.

Hearing the Decision

At the faculty meeting the chairman requested that each student be informed of his outcome by his advisor. Most students learned the result early that evening. Some, in fact, had learned of their outcomes before the meeting. In one case a faculty member confided in a student that, for all practical purposes, he had passed. In another case a faculty wife told an anxious student about the outcome while the faculty meeting was taking place. In some cases suggestions were made to students, unofficially, that they had done satisfactory work on the examinations. It may be that these leaks of early results are the "stuff" around which succeeding generations of students can build their defenses, for these leaks do suggest that decisions are made before the faculty have met and have gone over the results.

Most of the students, however, did not learn their

outcomes until after the faculty meeting. Some students waited in the building for the meeting to end so that they could see their advisors. Most of the others were phoned by their advisors. A few students reacted to hearing the result with almost a feeling of disbelief. Below is one student's description of his feelings at this time:

I was sort of calm until I hung up the phone and then I really felt good about it. An hour and a half or two after that, I started thinking real paranoid-like. "I'm not sure, I better call somebody else and find out about this for certain. . . . He said you passed the writtens without any trouble. What does this mean?" . . . I was really worried. I probably got more worried about it after he told me than I did before. . . . "This can't be true; or is it true? Or is someone tricking me."

The feelings described by this student are similar to those sometimes described by a person awaiting a very important decision, who has been holding tight reins on anxiety and aspiration level. When he hears the favorable result, he still seems to have a feeling of "residual anxiety" which takes some time to disappear. He may manifest this by becoming very concerned about confirmation, about possibilities that a mistake might have been made, or about a possible reversal of the result.

Most of the students looked toward hearing the decision that they had passed with considerable anticipation. They imagined that things would be different, that life now would be euphoric, and that all would be wonderful. A number of students, soon after hearing the result, experienced an empty, depressed feeling and found it difficult to return to work. Although students in their longing to be through with the examination situation saw a euphoric future, the post-examination period was not so experienced. The student's anticipation of the period after examinations was so favorable that a letdown was inevitable. This is somewhat similar to a reaction described by Grinker and Spiegel[2] of the combat soldier returning home:

As the neurotic and regressive reasons for the wish to go home increase, the concept of home becomes more unrealistic. As a haven from the dangers of combat with the enemy and from the threats of discipline on the part of superior officers in case of failure, home assumes the characteristics of a magical fairyland. All the faults and difficulties in the economic and social structure of the individual's home environment seem to fade away. The people at home become endowed with unrealistic attributes of beauty, kindness, generosity, and are considered to have the soldier's return home as their only desire. . . . At last, the soldier is home but in a peculiarly dissatisfied and often disturbed state of mind. This, of course, should be expected because his desires are unrealistic. No place or person in reality can reproduce his fantasies.

This "letdown" reaction appears to occur most intensively among students who tried to maintain strict control over their feelings of anxiety and who attempted to mask recognition of their feelings:

I don't feel quite as good as I thought I would. . . . I don't know why, but now that it's all over, it's just writtens.

Right [after hearing] I felt almost kind of depressed. I expected great joy, elation, ecstasy, or something, and right afterwards, for the first fifteen minutes, I felt sort of just flat; not really depressed, just flat. This tension has been building up for such a long time that, when it went away, it was kind of an empty feeling. . . .

That evening (the day of the faculty meeting) the students who already knew that they had passed, and some

2. R. R. Grinker and J. P. Spiegel, *Men Under Stress* (Philadelphia: Blakiston, 1945), pp. 184-185.

who had not yet spoken to their advisors, collected at the Central Building, congratulating one another and trying to piece together the fragments of information each had into the full story of what had taken place that afternoon at the faculty meeting. For example, it soon became obvious to the student that a change in procedure had occurred, that a new kind of deficiency system had been instituted. There was considerable talk about this and what it meant, as well as attempts to ascertain who it was who had passed with deficiencies. Various rumors concerning who had passed and who had failed traveled to and fro, and, as more and more information became available, rumors were modified.

Those who passed seemed to have learned of the result first, and most of those who had gathered at the Central Building already had learned that they had passed. The lack of presence of anyone who failed gave added confidence to some of the students who had not yet heard.

I thought I passed, especially when I found that [student *C*], [student *D*], and [student *E*] passed. . . . And when I did find out, it was quite a blow.

A feeling of social distance very quickly developed between those who had passed and those who had failed. Neither knew quite how to interact with the other, although passing students who had failed on previous attempts seemed to be more effective in interacting with those who failed than did second-year students. Especially among the second-year students, however, a desire for mutual avoidance developed. Neither the student who passed nor the student who failed knew how to approach the other; both, at least in the early days after examinations, attempted to avoid each other. The following state-

ment describes a situation the day after examination results were made public:

It was extremely uncomfortable . . . because [student G] was
there. He was a real good friend of mine and I was really
upset that he flunked. And I really didn't know what to do;
how to interact with him, how to approach him, or what. It
was quite uncomfortable. The thing that I did was that I just
feigned ignorance, that I didn't know anything about the
results. I did know all the results at the time. He was pretty
concerned about who passed and who failed. I just told him I
didn't know because I knew that he had been fairly convinced
that he had done quite a bit better than a number of people
taking it the second time, and yet these people had passed.
And I didn't want to be the one to tell him this. And he was
quite upset and quite depressed. . . . I was quite depressed the
whole day, and I really didn't know how to interact with him.

This was not an atypical response. Note the similarity
of some of the other responses of second-year students:

I kind of hope I don't run into them—because you think for
months and months about how you would feel if you failed,
and you just can't help to empathize so deeply with these
people. So it's sort of an edge off of your joy. You know how
important it is and what it means to these people. . . . It's just
such a sad thing that I wouldn't know what to say if I saw
a person like that. I wouldn't know whether to mention it, or
if they would feel that you are avoiding it, or feel bad either
way.

I really feel uncomfortable around [student O]. And it's hard
for me to talk to him. I have to kind of think of things to say.

This feeling was experienced by students who failed.
They also felt uncomfortable in interacting with other
students, as did their spouses.

Yesterday I went to class. . . . Maybe it bothers them as much
as it bothers me.

Yesterday, for instance, there was a wife's luncheon. [My wife] didn't want to go because the other wives would be there. It just made it real tough for her. . . . Then [student X and his wife] took her home and didn't say anything. . . . I just think I would come out and say something. Everybody would feel a lot better all the way around.

As the student statements show, students who passed felt rather badly about those who failed. In most cases the students did express sympathy for their friends who had not been successful.

I'm very sorry that some people didn't make it. This sort of puts a sting into the victory. . . . [A student who failed] seemed pretty upset. He shook his head and he didn't take any notes in class. He waited until everybody else had left before he left the class.

The intense sympathy the student develops for those who fail is in part a defense against his own fleeting thought in which he obtains gratification from others' failures. One student, for example, expressed considerable resentment that others who had not studied equally as hard as he had passed; this was followed, however, by an indication of extreme regret for those who had failed. Thus, this feeling of intense sympathy in part may represent a way of hiding one's own feeling of being victorious in departmental competition.

The students who became visibly upset by the failures of others they knew were the older students who had gone through the experience themselves and who could, therefore, empathize considerably with those who had failed. It was these students, as has been indicated, who were most effective at interacting with others who failed.

After the students who passed had learned the results, their feelings toward the examinations became more friendly, although by no means did the student shift to a position of unqualified approval. It is likely that the process through which students develop more favorable attitudes toward examinations is, if it does occur, a relatively slow one. But, already one week following examinations, some of the second-year students were beginning to experience a shift in feelings about the examinations.

I'm glad they have writtens now. . . . It's kind of a feeling of accomplishment if you do get through them. Also it points out your adequacies and inadequacies more strongly than if you were just left to your own devices.

I feel that it was a very worthwhile experience, regardless of the results. Whether I passed or failed, I would have felt the same way. The main reason I thought it was worthwhile was in terms of the amount of work it made me do. It gave me contact with subject matter, which, without it, I might not have gotten contact with. But, perhaps, more important from a personal point of view . . . it gave me a chance to sort of observe my reactions in a situation which I, hitherto, had not come across. It was illuminating in some respects and discouraging in some others. . . . I'm a little more aware of myself now, of my limitations and capacities, than six months ago. And, in terms of passing, it's a boost to my ego which I think I sort of needed. It was a real worthwhile thing, but I wouldn't want to take it over again. I wouldn't want to go through it again.

Students who had gone through the examination experience twice were not as rapid in mellowing. In the questionnaires administered approximately four weeks following examinations, some of the students who had passed on the second attempt still retained, although perhaps somewhat less strongly, a hostile picture of examinations.

I still have a strong feeling that the examination procedure is inadequate as an evaluation device.

There has been some relaxation of tension, but a considerable amount of resentment still exists. My opinion of the faculty members and examination process has not changed materially.

Although some mellowing in student attitudes could be noted, four weeks following examinations they still retained many of their pre- and during-examination attitudes. It is likely, however, that as time passes the saliency of the situation will decrease sufficiently and attitudes will change. It is unlikely, however, that the students who have had to go through the process twice will remember it with great delight. In some ways the process resembles army experience: going through it might make one likely to talk of his experiences years later with some satisfaction, but it does not necessarily lead to a favorable opinion of the experience.

Reaction to Failure

Failure on the examinations seemed to lead to either of two reactions, both having as their basis a considerable loss in self-esteem and esteem in the eyes of others. Some students experienced a feeling of utter humiliation; others felt a great surge of hostility toward the examination process and toward the examiners. Still other students fluctuated between the two reactions. The second reaction—anger-out—seems to have been a defense against the discomfort of the first reaction—humiliation (or anger-in).

The Anger-in Reaction

In this reaction the student primarily blamed himself for his failure, and he felt intensely ashamed, humiliated, and upset. One of the students under study had such a reaction: he felt crushed; he did not want to see or talk with others. At the same time he felt that the examinations had been objective and that the subjective feelings of the faculty had not played a prime role in their decision. However, interviews with older students indicated that the anger-in reaction usually would change eventually to an anger-out reaction.

The Anger-out Reaction

The more prevalent anger-out reaction seemed more likely to occur when the student was very highly involved in the situation. Thus its incidence was higher among older students than younger ones. In this reaction—a protective covering by which the student defends against threatening and humiliating thoughts—he becomes so involved in his anger that it serves as a protective device against self-questioning and self-blame. Instead of feeling humiliation, the student feels outraged; he projects himself as an object and victim of injustice and wrongdoing.

THE ANTICIPATORY ANGER-OUT REACTION. When students sensed that they had performed badly on the examinations and were expecting failure, some developed anticipatory anger-out reactions.

I had given [student X] a ride home Friday afternoon after the last examination. He was cursing and was very upset about the kind of questions they had asked. And I had the feeling, then, that there was something about him . . . that he was just not going to make it.

Another student who expected that he had failed described his attitudes toward the examinations and faculty:

In [area L] I didn't get finished. I got two questions done and

then time was up. I didn't have time to write any more. I
didn't really feel too bad about it. That was a stupid question
. . . I couldn't care less . . . I felt that way about several of
the questions actually . . . I just don't care about these things.
. . . [In regard to the department decision-making process] I
find the whole business of secrecy kind of appalling. It's like
nobody knows their own mind. They have to all get together
before anybody knows what they think. It seems to me that
anybody working here . . . should, at least, by now know me
[well enough] to have a pretty good idea of what they think
of my potential. . . . But nobody will tell me. They have to
wait for the other people to tell them, just on the basis of
these examinations. That seems to me quite irrational.

ANGER-OUT AFTER THE DECISION. The student who fails
the examinations may attempt to find outside "nonobjective" factors which account for his situation.

[Student C] is blaming others than himself for his failure to
get through. . . . Apparently he feels that he didn't fail to pass
because of knowledge but because of personal factors. . . . He
has been quite bitter toward the University, and the department in particular.

As the reader will remember, we have already given a
number of examples of the anger-out reaction in the early
discussion of the attitudes expressed by students who had
failed on prior attempts. Since so little data are available
on the members of the group under study who failed, the
early discussion will have to suffice.

After Examinations

After examinations end and the results are known,
students find that there is still much to do. Although there
is a substantial diminution of anxiety and tension, things
have not changed very much. Master's theses must be

completed, dissertation proposals suggested, language examinations passed, and so on. And, while these tasks do not have the urgency of examinations, they do constitute barriers to be passed, and the student soon realizes that work must go on as always.

Yet most students experienced great difficulty in returning to work. They found it hard to engender sufficient motivation to undertake other than routine intellectual tasks. Thus, the period after examinations was experienced as an anticlimax, and many students reported mental fatigue, loss of motivation, and restlessness.

The students who experienced the most extreme restless feelings were those who had studied hardest for examinations. Some of the students who did less studying experienced even greater ability to work than before. The common feeling was one of apathy. Listed below are some student comments made approximately four weeks after examinations.

Since hearing the outcome of examinations, it has been quite difficult to get back to work. Somehow, everything seems pretty anticlimatic. I hope I will be able to start being more productive in the near future. It seems that all my plans were put off until after writtens and now that they are all over, it's hard to get started again.

My motivation to work has also dropped. I think it will take several months for me to feel ready to work with a full load of steam.

I am presently suffering from a boredom with all of [the field]. I hope it goes away soon. Anxiety and thought of examinations are gone. Ability to work is close to nothing. I feel that I'm filled up to the brim with [the field] and that I don't want any more. It seems uninteresting now.

It has been difficult since that time to descend from my cloud and again begin working. Although my enthusiasm for [the field] has not decreased, my motivation to actually start working again has diminished appreciably.

Students who have made less of a studying effort usually do not experience this reaction or, if they do, not very intensely. The following remark was made by one of the students who had studied casually for examinations: "Generally, I've been much more able to organize my work, so that I can accomplish much more in less time. At the same time, there has been a tendency to relax a bit."

As we have described the main reactions of students before, during, and after taking the preliminary doctoral examinations, we now shall proceed to a discussion of stress research in general, to be followed by a summary of the theoretical significance of this study.

10
THE CONTEXT OF
STRESS RESEARCH

THE PRESENTATION thus far has been highly descriptive. It is now necessary to develop more carefully the theoretical implications of this study and to indicate its place within the context of stress research. Moreover, it is valuable to suggest implications that have bearing on further research on stress and adaptation. However, before discussing the particular significance of this study, it is necessary that we review the concept of stress, its meaning for different areas of investigation, and some of its empirical implications.

The term *stress* has come to sociology by way of the physical and biological sciences, and, in its wider sense, has been applied generally to disruptions in personal, social, and cultural processes that have some relationship to problems of health and disease. Biologists, biochemists, physicians, psychoanalysts, social psychologists, and sociologists—all have been interested in this notion. Thus, the study of stress has brought together research and findings from many disciplines and points of view. It would be an impossible task to review fully all of the various stress studies that have been completed. What is especially relevant for the understanding of our problem is to see how the many stress research activities relate to one another. In the following sections we will review the notions of stress and adaptation as they are used in medicine, in ego psychology, in social psychology, and in the analysis of social systems.

The Stress Concept in Medicine

Although there has been a long history of the attempt to use hypnosis in the healing arts—to affect the body by way of the mind—it was not until well into the present century that any systematic effort was made to investigate the effects of such mental states as fear, rage, and anxiety upon body processes. And only in very recent years have such efforts been granted the recognition of a special designation—psychosomatic medicine. This recognition of the effects of mental states on body processes not only instigated a general abandonment of the artificial distinction between mind and body but also opened the way for the inclusion of the behavioral sciences—specifically psychology and sociology—as contributors to the field of medicine. The rationale for the inclusion of the findings of psychology and sociology in the science of medicine is now fairly clear: the mental condition—the personality—of the patient does have bearing upon the appearance and course of illness, and, in turn, his mental state is largely if not exclusively a product of his position in his society and how he perceives it.

In recent years the relationship between physical "stress" and illness has been given considerable attention in scientific literature, largely as a consequence of the work of Hans Selye.[1] An endocrinologist and biochemist, Selye has described a vital stress mechanism in the organism as a result of his experiments on animals. He has described what he calls the General Adaptation Syndrome (G.A.S.) as developing in three stages: the alarm reaction; the stage of resistance; and the stage of exhaustion. Exposure of the organism to a *stressor*—which, in Selye's terms, may be extremes of temperature or some toxic substance—brings on the alarm reaction to counteract it. *Resistance* refers to those internal responses which stimulate tissue defense. If the condition brought about by the stressor persists, the stage of exhaustion is eventually reached, followed either by extensive damage to the organism or death. In brief, the G.A.S. mechanism indicates stress, that is, the "wear and tear" on the body; and, when the G.A.S. reactions are not properly balanced, they often result in "diseases of adaptation." He writes:

A state can be recognized only by its manifestations; for instance, the state of stress by the manifestations of the stress syndrome. Therefore, you have to observe a great many living beings exposed to a variety of agents before you can see the shape and stress as such. Those changes which are specifically induced by only one or the other agent must first be rejected: if you take what is left—that which is nonspecifically induced by many agents—you have unveiled the picture of stress itself. This picture is the G.A.S. Once this is established, you can recognize stress no matter where it turns up; indeed, you can

1. H. Selye, *The Stress of Life* (New York: McGraw-Hill Book Co., Inc., 1956).

even measure it by the intensity of the G.A.S.-manifestations which it produces.[2]

In his experimental work Selye observed that the stress process was accompanied by adrenocortical enlargement, atrophy of the thymicolymphatic organs, gastro-intestinal ulceration, loss in body weight, the disappearance of eosinophil cells from the blood, and a number of chemical alterations in the constitution of body fluids and tissues.

Although Selye's work has been at the biochemical and physiological level of adaptation, his findings have suggested that psychosocial factors may be able to initiate the stress syndrome in a manner similar to physical stimuli. In recent years a number of investigations have been undertaken on the basis of this assumption. There appear to be two principal approaches—the psychoanalytic and the life situation.

THE PSYCHOANALYTIC APPROACH. One of the leading theoreticians of the psychoanalytic school—Franz Alexander[3]—holds that emotional factors play a major role in hysterical conversion symptoms, vegetative neuroses, and organic disease. The *conversion symptom* is viewed as an attempt to relieve an emotional tension that can find no other adequate symbolic expression. The *vegetative neurosis* is looked upon as a psychologically induced dysfunction of an organ concomitant with the emotional tension. If, according to Alexander, the vegetative neurosis persists it may result in permanent structural damage.

The basic assumption of the psychoanalytic approach is that stress can manifest itself in a number of linked open systems. Stress that occurs in one system may be transferred to others so that several systems may play a

2. *Ibid.*, pp. 54-55.

3. F. Alexander, *Psychosomatic Medicine: Its Principles and Applications* (New York: W. W. Norton and Co., 1950).

part in the adaptive process. Roy Grinker,[4] for example, another proponent of the psychoanalytic school, believes that generalized infantile anxiety can become conditioned to certain fragmentary visceral patterns. In early life these may be functionally adaptive to specific stressors as the physiological expression of homeostatic disturbance; but in later life anxiety becomes intensified for various reasons and the old pattern reappears. Excessive occurrence of this infantile pattern, while it may be adaptive, can result in disease. Grinker has posited a transactional view of five systems: the enzymatic system including the hormones; the organ systems; the nervous system; the psychological system; and the sociocultural system. When a given system is strained in handling a particular stressor, the minor preparatory changes in a related system become intensified and apparent as another response to the initial stimulus. Grinker sees this integration of systems as inherent in both the preparatory activity and in the more intense reaction to "stress stimuli" impinging on any one of them. Integration within any system is dependent upon its capacity to act alone without strain before action in another system is initiated. When anxiety becomes too intense, disruptive effects ensue, bringing forth emergency substitutive mechanisms of defense (the intervention of other systems).

In both of the foregoing theories early childhood experiences are assumed to provide "explanations" of later psychosomatic disorders. Both theories therefore are scientifically inadequate since it is impossible to demonstrate empirically that an individual's early life experiences are in fact responsible for physiological changes that occur in later life.

THE LIFE SITUATION APPROACH. In some respects the

4. R. R. Grinker, *Psychosomatic Research* (New York: W. W. Norton and Co., 1953).

life situation approach is similar to the psychoanalytic, but it has a different emphasis. This approach has been reflected in the writings and research of Harold Wolff and associates,[5] who show that noxious substances applied to the body will call forth offensive and defensive reactions in the organism. In this respect their work has paralleled that of Selye. But Wolff and his associates also have demonstrated that such reactions can be generalized from *physically* threatening life situations to *socially* threatening life situations, such as loss of status, loss of security, or unsatisfactory interpersonal relations. When such conditioned responses occur frequently—in a variety of situations perceived to be socially or personally defeating—symptom formation and tissue damage can result.

The two views of social stress and physiological response described above do not, of course, encompass all the specific concepts of this relationship to be found in the literature.[6] But many of the important theories regarding

5. The works of Wolff and his associates have been widely reported and the following is a sample of volumes where they may be found. Emphasis is placed on experimental findings. H. G. Wolff, *Stress and Disease* (Springfield: Charles C Thomas, 1953): *Proc. A. Research Nerv. and Ment. Dis., Life Stress and Bodily Disease* (Baltimore: Williams and Wilkins, 1950); L. Simmons and H. G. Wolff, *Social Science in Medicine* (New York: Russell Sage Foundation, 1954); A. Weider (ed.), *Contributions Toward Medical Psychology,* Vol. I (New York: Ronald Press Co., 1953); H. G. Wolff, "Disease and the Patterns of Behavior," in E. G. Jaco (ed.), *Patients, Physicians and Illness* (New York: The Free Press of Glencoe, 1958); H. G. Wolff, "Stress and Adaptive Patterns Resulting in Tissue Damage in Man," in *The Medical Clinics of North America* (Philadelphia: W. B. Saunders, 1955), pp. 783-797; L. E. Hinkle, Jr. and H. G. Wolff, "Health and the Social Environment: Experimental Investigations," in A. H. Leighton, J. A. Clausen, and R. N. Wilson (eds.), *Explorations in Social Psychiatry* (New York: Basic Books, 1957); L. E. Hinkle, Jr. and N. Plummer, "Life Stress and Industrial Absenteeism," *Industrial Medicine and Surgery, 21,* 1952, 363-375; H. G. Wolff, "Stress, Emotions and Bodily Disease," in I. Galdston (ed.), *Medicine and Science* (New York: International Universities Press, 1954) pp. 94-131.

6. From a historical point of view the following three works are important: H. F. Dunbar, *Emotions and Bodily Changes* (New York: Columbia

this relationship do seem to be built upon assumptions similar to those already discussed. The principal advantage of Wolff's approach is that his conceptualizations and operational research procedures are closely related, and that in this sense his methods more closely approximate ideal scientific canons than do those of the psychoanalytic theorists.

Psychosomatic reactions to social stress have been investigated in various contexts. A few examples will suffice. Ruesch[7] found that social "strivers" who fail to gain the prestige they seek often are afflicted with psychosomatic complaints. Wolf and Wolff,[8] studying a gastric fistula patient, observed gastric hyperactivity during periods when the patient faced ordinary life situations that either frustrated him or evoked his anger and hostility. And, after an extensive review of the literature and study of the ulcer patient, Sullivan and McKell concluded that:

It is our belief that this intensive drive and the tension it creates as well as the inborn craving for superiority, together with the worries generated by small failures, particularly the anxiety resulting from anticipated failure or future insecurity, are the emotional patterns which are fundamental in the production of ulcer.[9]

Treuting and Ripley,[10] observing fifty-six patients over a

University Press, 1954); E. Weiss and O. S. English, *Psychosomatic Medicine* (Philadelphia: W. B. Saunders, 1943); and J. L. Halliday, *Psychosocial Medicine: A Study of the Sick Society* (New York: W. W. Norton and Co., 1948).

7. J. Ruesch, "Social Technique, Social Status and Social Change in Illness," in C. Kluckhohn and H. Murray (eds.), *Personality in Nature, Society and Culture* (New York: Alfred A. Knopf, 1948), pp. 117-130.

8. S. Wolf and H. G. Wolff, *Human Gastric Function: An Experimental Study of a Man and His Stomach* (New York: Oxford University Press, 1943).

9. A. J. Sullivan and T. E. McKell, *Personality in Peptic Ulcer* (Springfield: Charles C Thomas, 1950), p. 46.

10. Reported in M. Hamilton, *Psychosomatics* (New York: John Wiley and Sons, Inc., 1955), p. 35.

long period, found that attacks of asthma were related to the patients' emotional reactions to life situations. Hinkle and Wolff[11] found that illness was associated with occupational and social conditions that frustrated the needs and aspirations of the individuals under study.

Many of the psychosomatic studies are methodologically inadequate. Often these studies rely totally on casual observations and too few investigators employ controls.[12] However, the relationship between stress and physiological response has been documented clearly, and there seems to be little doubt that such relationships do exist, although the complexity of physiological response to stress is yet to be unraveled. Also, while there is considerable evidence that stress is associated with some illnesses, the role of stress in many specific illnesses has continued to be a controversial matter.

Ego Psychology and the Mechanisms of Defense

Psychoanalysts and clinical psychologists attempt to account for behavior in situations of perceived threat through a theory of ego psychology that views adaptation in terms of a number of defense mechanisms. The basic approach to defense processes stems from the work of Sigmund Freud and his daughter Anna Freud. In 1894 Freud used the term *defense* to refer to the efforts of the person to protect himself against instinctual demands and conflicts arising in human development. In 1926, in his dis-

11. Hinkle, Jr., and Wolff in Leighton *et al., op. cit.*

12. See D. Mechanic and E. H. Volkart, "Stress, Illness Behavior and the Sick Role," *American Sociological Review, 26* (February, 1961), 51-58; *ibid.,* "Illness Behavior and Medical Diagnosis," *Journal of Health and Human Behavior, 1* (Summer, 1960), 86-94.

cussion of "The Problem of Anxiety," Freud wrote that defense "shall be the general designation for all the techniques of which the ego makes use in the conflicts which potentially lead to neurosis."[13] In 1936 Anna Freud elaborated on the defense mechanisms, listing nine such defenses used by the ego under pressure of excessive anxiety: regression, repression, reaction-formation, isolation, undoing, projection, introjection, turning against the self, and reversal. The defense mechanisms all have two things in common: they deny, falsify, or distort reality; they operate unconsciously so that the person is not aware of what is taking place.[14]

The defense mechanisms as first described were closely linked with Freud's theory of biological instincts. Thus the defense mechanisms were posed as the solution to fundamental instinctual problems inherent in the human biological structure. Defense was seen as the manner in which the organism dealt with the inevitable conflict between biological needs and the expectations of society.

As first presented, the mechanisms of defense were viewed as unhealthy solutions to life problems. The neurotic rather than the normal functions of defense were emphasized. But the mechanisms of defense have long since been used more as descriptive categories to characterize behavior than as important theoretical concepts. Later psychoanalysts—for example, Horney[15]—removed the theory of defense from instinct theory and viewed defense as the solution to conflicts engendered by the social environment. The study of defenses in emphasizing de-

13. Quoted in Ruth L. Munroe, *Schools of Psychoanalytic Thought* (New York: Dryden Press, 1955), p. 91.

14. C. S. Hall and G. Lindzey, *Theories of Personality* (New York: John Wiley and Sons, Inc., 1957).

15. *Ibid.,* Chap. 4.

scriptions of behavior has had a valuable function in sensitizing investigators to certain important human events.

A number of investigators have used the psychoanalytic framework of defense in stress studies. Grinker and
Spiegel,[16] for example, utilized psychodynamic principles
to explain the breakdown of flying personnel under battle
conditions. In a more recent study Janis[17] attempted to
account for attitudes toward impending surgery by using
psychoanalytic principles. Bettelheim[18] used similar principles to account for behavior in the concentration camp,
as did Cohen.[19] In fact, much of the research linking stress
and behavior has been undertaken within the psychoanalytic framework of defense.[20]

While these studies have made a considerable contribution to the study of stress, emphasizing intrapsychic
processes as they do, they have failed to explore many of
the social contingencies of stress situations. It is within
this area that the social psychologist and sociologist can
make a contribution to stress research.

The Social-Psychological Framework
for Stress Research

There have been a number of studies of the effects of
stress situations on behavior reported in the social-psychological literature. These studies, however, have had no

---

16. R. R. Grinker and J. P. Spiegel, *Men Under Stress* (New York:
McGraw-Hill Book Co., Inc., 1945).

17. I. L. Janis, *Psychological Stress* (New York: John Wiley and Sons,
Inc., 1958).

18. B. Bettelheim, "Individual and Mass Behavior in Extreme Situations," *J. Abnorm. Soc. Psychol., 38,* 1943, 417-452.

19. E. A. Cohen, *Human Behavior in the Concentration Camp* (New
York: W. W. Norton and Co., 1953).

20. For example, see the bibliography in Janis, *op. cit.,* pp. 413-430.

central theoretical framework; some have stemmed from concern with cognitive consistency and clarity,[21] others from study of marginal roles, prison groups, reactions to deprivation, brainwashing, and the like.[22] In many of these studies, however, a set of assumptions has been made that stem from Thomas' early concern with crisis and the definition of the situation.

THOMAS' CONCEPT OF CRISIS. Thomas fused the notion of *crisis* with his "concept of the definition of the situation." As long as social life runs smoothly, he believed, and as long as habits are adjustive, *situations* do not exist. There

---

21. See, for example, Leon Festinger, *A Theory of Cognitive Dissonance* (Evanston: Row, Peterson and Company, 1957).

22. The attempts to deal with stressful life demands have been described by various mechanisms: a closely supervised informal set of norms to counteract formal demands—N. Hayner and E. Ash, "The Prison as a Community," *Amer. Sociological Rev., 5,* 1940, 577-583; C. Bondy, "Problems of Internment Camps," *J. Abnorm. Soc. Psychol., 38,* 1943, 453-457; aggression or its displacement—J. Dollard, L. Doob, N. Miller, O. Mowrer, and R. Sears, *Frustration and Aggression* (New Haven: Yale University Press, 1939); G. W. Allport, *The Nature of Prejudice* (Cambridge: Addison-Wesley, 1954); G. E. Simpson and J. M. Yinger, *Racial and Cultural Minorities* (New York: Harper and Bros., 1953), pp. 182-188; Cohen, *op. cit.;* deviant forms of behavior—Simpson and Yinger, *op. cit.;* self-aggression and aggression against one's group—K. Lewin, *Resolving Social Conflicts* (New York: Harper and Bros., 1948); humor—E. H. Schein, "The Chinese Indoctrination Program for Prisoners of War," *Psychiatry, 19,* 1956, 149-172; Cohen, *op. cit.;* Simpson and Yinger, *op. cit.;* D. Hamburg, "Psychological Adaptive Processes in Life-Threatening Injuries," *Symposium on Stress* (Washington-National Research Council and Walter Reed Army Medical Center, 1953); chauvinistic and ethnocentric behaviors—Allport, *op. cit.;* Simpson and Yinger, *op. cit.;* increased time perspective—K. Lewin, *op. cit.;* substitution—Bettelheim, *op. cit.;* Simpson and Yinger, *op. cit.;* physical and emotional withdrawal—E. H. Schein, "Some Observations on Chinese Methods of Handling Prisoners of War," *Public Opinion Quarterly, 20,* 1956, 321-327; Schein, *op. cit.;* Bettelheim, *op. cit.;* Simpson and Yinger, *op. cit.;* M. Sherif and H. Cantril, *The Psychology of Ego-Involvements* (New York: John Wiley and Sons, Inc., 1947); regression—Schein, "The Chinese Indoctrination Program for Prisoners of War," *op. cit.;* Cohen, *op. cit.;* Bettelheim, *op. cit.;* and denial—Cohen, *op. cit.;* D. Hamburg, Beatrix Hamburg, and S. deGoza, "Adaptive Problems and Mechanisms in Severely Burned Patients," *Psychiatry, 16,* 1953, 1-20.

is nothing to define when people have anticipated ways of responding. However, when habits become disrupted, new stimuli demand attention, and, when the usual situation is altered, we then have the roots of a "crisis."[23]

Thomas believed that adjustment and control resulted from the individual's ability to compare a present situation with similar ones in the past and to revise judgments and actions in light of past experience.[24]

The behavior of an individual as social personality is not scientifically reducible to sensually observable movements and cannot be explained on the grounds of the direct experience of the observing psychologist; the movements (including words) must be interpreted in terms of intentions, desires, emotions, etc.—in a word, in terms of attitudes—and the explanation of any particular act of personal behavior must be sought on the ground of the experience of the behaving individual which the observer has indirectly to reconstruct by way of conclusions from what is directly given to him. We cannot neglect the meanings, the suggestions which objects have for the conscious individual, because it is these meanings which determine the individual's behavior; and we cannot explain these meanings as mere abbreviations of the individual's past acts of biological adaptation to his material environment—as manifestations of organic memory—because the meanings to which he reacts are not only those which material things have assumed for him as a result of his own past organic activities, but also those which these things have acquired long ago in society and which the individual is taught to understand during his whole education as conscious member of a social group.[25]

Harold Wolff, the proponent of the life situation approach, has a similar point of view. He writes:

---

23. E. H. Volkart (ed.), *Social Behavior and Personality* (New York: Social Science Research Council, 1951), p. 12.

24. *Ibid.*, p. 218.

25. *Ibid.*, pp. 155-156.

The stress accruing from a situation is based in large part on the way the affected subject perceives it—perception depends upon a multiplicity of factors including the genetic equipment, basic individual needs and longings, earlier conditioning influences, and a host of life experiences and cultural pressures. No one of these can be singled out for exclusive emphasis. The common denominator of stress disorders is reaction to circumstances of threatening significance to the organism.[26]

The approach we have taken in describing the department studied is basically simple: people react to situations in terms of socially acquired ends and the means available to them for accomplishing these goals. Threat responses occur when people are motivated toward ends but meet barriers in their acquisition. These barriers may result from faulty perception, faulty learning, or the realistic demands or newness of the situation. As Weber has written: ". . . our physical existence and the satisfaction of our most ideal needs are everywhere confronted with the quantitative limits and the qualitative inadequacy of the necessary external means, so that satisfaction requires planful provision of work, struggle with nature, and the association of human beings."[27]

The Relevance
of Social System Analysis
for Stress Research

In recent years there has been increasing concern with discontinuities in social systems resulting in stress re-

26. Wolff, "Life Situations, Emotions and Bodily Disease," in *Symposium on Stress* (Washington: National Research Council and Walter Reed Army Medical Center, 1953), p. 133.

27. Max Weber, *The Methodology of the Social Sciences* (New York: The Free Press of Glencoe, 1949), p. 64.

sponses. Merton[28] has argued that social structures exert definite pressures upon certain persons in the society forcing them to make such deviant adaptations as innovation, ritualism, retreatism, and rebellion. In short, when an acute incongruency develops between the cultural norms and goals and the socially structured capacities of persons to behave in accord with them, a state of anomie exists. Individuals who learn cultural goals and values, but who fail to acquire the means to fulfill these because of their location within the society, adapt to these anomic conditions by making the deviant adaptations described by Merton. Thus the deviant adaptation is structurally produced. Cohen[29] has argued that delinquent subcultures result in part from structurally induced failure, made more humiliating by the American belief that "man should make something of himself." Others have attributed various forms of personal deviance to social disorganization, urbanization, rapid social change, and the like.[30]

Still another area of social systems research concerns the network of social expectations. Because of the complexity of social life, persons often are faced with conflicting or contradictory demands. Role conflict theorists[31] have been concerned with describing and predicting the adaptations that persons make when faced with these demands. Stress responses may be socially induced when persons are faced with incompatible demands which they

---

28. R. Merton, *Social Theory and Social Structure* (New York: The Free Press of Glencoe, 1957), pp. 131-194.

29. Albert K. Cohen, *Delinquent Boys, The Culture of the Gang* (New York: The Free Press of Glencoe, 1955).

30. See, for example, Marshall Clinard, *Sociology of Deviant Behavior* (New York: Holt, Rinehart & Winston, 1957).

31. See, for example, Jackson Toby, "Some Variables in Role Conflict Analysis," *Social Forces, 30,* 1952, 324-327.

consider equally legitimate and to which they can not easily adjust.

From the larger structural point of view it is quite possible to study not only responses to discontinuities, but also the discontinuities themselves that are likely to induce stress in particular groups of persons, and factors that condition the adaptive solutions attempted. Although the hazards of studying stress situations have been discussed, we have pointed at various times in our descriptive treatment of the department studied to factors in the system of interaction that did increase the stress experience of some of the students studied.

As this chapter has attempted to show, stress has been studied on the levels of social, cultural, psychological, and physiological systems, and, at various points, these views have converged. What links these various inquiries is that they all in one way or another have been concerned with symbolic behavior. In our description of the department studied, symbolic behavior has been emphasized: the various definitions of the situation, communication, symbolic defense, and the like. Furthermore, we have tried to deal with stress, not as an event, but as a *response*, depending on the meanings attributed to various aspects of the social situation. But whether we speak of physiological response to threat or socially adaptive behaviors, we must take into account how the individual views his situation and the relevance of his view for his response.

11
CONCLUSION

STRESS HAS RECEIVED considerable attention in previous research. But these studies have primarily emphasized "flight" processes, rather than the more usual attempts that persons make to deal satisfactorily with challenging situations. Thus we have a considerable literature on "irrational defense," but relatively little on "rational defense"; many studies on stress and physiological change, stress and illness, and so on, but almost none on what people under stress actively do to remedy their situations.

Stress situations are not qualitatively different from *nonstress* or *nonthreat* situations. All of them to some extent require response. But in many situations the responses required are easily learned and easily effected, so that all but the "mentally retarded" and "physically handicapped" take them for granted. There are occasions, however, where persons are faced with situations where the necessary responses are difficult for all or most people and cannot readily be made. These situations may be especially difficult because they require efforts above the usual capacities of the normal person, or because the group's experience offers no effective means for dealing with them. Situations like tornadoes, bombings, floods, and earthquakes are likely to be threatening to most who encounter them.

On the societal level a stress situation is one in which most people either have insufficient means to deal with the situation or, if sufficient means are available, lack the capacity to manipulate them effectively. Thus we can view stress situations from two perspectives: first, from the number of people who have difficulty in reversing the situation effectively; second, from the extent to which individuals have difficulty in reversing the situation. The first perspective defines what we might or might not consider stress situations. The second in part defines the magnitude of stress situations for particular persons. A situation that requires adaptation but one that the actor cannot reverse is, from his personal point of view, a stress situation.

The difficulty an individual experiences in a situation or his stress reaction to a situation is dependent on the extent to which means can or cannot easily be brought to bear in reversing the challenge, the extent to which the situation persists and demands attention *(duration),* and the individual's involvement in the situation *(importance).* Among our student group, involvement was dependent on the extent of commitment (in time and self-esteem) and on the costs of making this commitment (finances, marriage demands and the like).

The key concept we utilized was *adaptation,* defined in this study as the manner in which the individual comes to terms with his situation. The person who attempts to adapt to a situation is faced with a two-fold problem: he must be able to deal with the situation, and he must orient himself to utilizing what means he can to reverse it. If the situation is a difficult one the person is likely to become afraid, anxious, depressed, and upset; and, to the extent that these feelings interfere, his effectiveness as a coper is limited. If he is to deal most effectively with the task he faces, he must in some manner control uncomfortable interfering stimuli and maintain relative comfort or integration. This process we call *defense*. Adequate adaptation depends on some careful balance between coping and defense processes.

Although the study of combat stress by Grinker and Spiegel was oriented around principles of psychodynamics, they did recognize at various points the importance of both the problems of coping and defense. They write:

In combat, the object which is chiefly threatened is the life and existence of the individual. Although, as we have shown, there are other sources of anxiety, this is probably the most acute. The reaction to the stimuli of combat depends upon the meaning given to these stimuli in terms of recognizing them as a threat and of feeling confident of the ability to neutralize the threat. Both of these are matters of interpretation based on past experience, and, when this has been a bad experience in which the ego has found itself dependent and defenseless, anxiety is liberated. Neurotic anxiety is therefore a last-ditch emergency mechanism biologically oriented toward a flight from the threatening situation. However, other forces, located in the superego or in the external environment, demand a continued attempt to master the threat, and at their behest the ego attempts to inhibit or control the anxiety.[1]

In short, adaptation requires that the individual be able to bring means to bear so as to satisfactorily achieve

---

1. R. R. Grinker and J. P. Spiegel, *Men Under Stress* (New York: McGraw-Hill Book Co., Inc., 1945), p. 141.

some result, both in regard to his functioning and to his inner security. From a societal point of view, mechanisms must exist for obtaining means; from the personal point of view, the individual must have the capacity to control and manipulate them. Thus, although the group usually will provide some appropriate paths for facilitating adaptation, the individual must learn to use these paths effectively. For example, the academic department offers courses to learn specialized techniques and other information, but the student must have the ability and expend the effort to learn the appropriate materials.

The study reported here was begun with the contention that the social environment is an important variable in adaptation—that it is the community that sets the limits, provides the alternatives, and defines the meanings to be attached to various situations. Once again Grinker and Spiegel also came to a similar conclusion, although they chose to deemphasize it. They first pointed out that in combat situations the soldier to a large extent must surrender his individuality to the combat group. He then becomes highly dependent on the combat group not only because he acts as part of a team, but also because of the nature of the combat situation itself. They write:

The combat personality surrenders a great deal of its freedom of activity to the group, which is then relied upon for protection. The efficient functioning of the team is the guarantee of safety, and this applies equally to the efficient functioning of equipment, such as the aircraft, which must be maintained by teams. As long as the group demonstrates its ability to master the dangers fairly effectively, the individual feels sufficiently protected and competent in the environment. But when combat losses are high and close friends have been lost, or when the individual has experienced repeated narrow escapes or a traumatic event, the group is no longer a good security, and the ego learns how helpless it is in the situation.[2]

This statement can easily apply to a student group taking Ph.D. examinations. The means, as Grinker and Spiegel have noted, are not only personal but include also the equipment available to the group, whether airplanes, books, or old examinations. In a sense the student like the soldier becomes committed to his group and highly dependent upon it. To the extent that the rate of past failures on examinations is very low, students can feel considerable security that they also will pass; but should the rate of failures in the department be high, and close friends of equal competence fail to make the grade, the student then feels less secure about the situation and his future.

Both coping and defense techniques are restricted considerably by normative controls from the full range of adaptive possibilities. For example, the student taking Ph.D. examinations is not left to his own devices. How he deals with the examinations is restricted by rules: he may not cheat; he may not utilize books and notes or consult with others during the examinations; he may not have someone else take the examinations for him; and so forth. The environment, however, also provides a variety of alternatives for dealing with his situation: he may take or audit courses; he may discuss the examinations with professors; he may study, using old examinations; or he may request reading lists. While perhaps not as obvious, defensive techniques also are restricted. Should the defensive device become too bizarre, it is likely to be defined as deviant and result in various pressures and sanctions. Thus the student will attempt to seek external validation for the

2. *Ibid.*, p. 129.

beliefs and attitudes that serve as his defenses. To the extent that his manner of dealing with his feelings is either visibly bizarre or interferes with adequate coping, the consequences of his behavior may become a serious problem.

For this reason, the student must select from available legitimate adaptive devices. He must allocate his time in order to plan his adaptive scheme in light of what he regards as his own strengths and weaknesses. He cannot read all the books relevant to his areas and take all the courses offered, nor can he fully release himself from other demands on his time (assistantships, family, and the like). Thus he must strategize and appropriate his means toward what he sees as the most important and difficult aspects of the task.

The students under study had no fully rational basis for allocating their efforts and abilities toward the task in one way rather than another. They attempted to gauge their behavior by observing those around them and their behavior vis-à-vis the task. Through the process of social comparison the student not only anticipated the capability of his orientation to his situation, but also the progress he was making toward an adequate preparation. Indications that his preparation was not adequate, or that his manipulation of the necessary means was not satisfactory, stimulated his discomfort. Thus he became upset when, in his estimation, he compared unfavorably in his studying progress with other students like himself, or found that he was unable to concentrate, study, or use important means in an adequate fashion.

Since the student is part of a group, and because he estimates his progress by social comparison within the context of group competition, communication is a crucial factor in the study of stress situations. The information the student has available, the means he considers, and the means he uses are all dependent in part on his position within the structure of communication of which he is a member. His physical location will affect the rate of his communication, and this, in turn, will affect what he learns about various alternatives for coping and defense.

Communication, however, also has disadvantages. While communication does increase information and facilitate coping, it often can present new problems of defense, as the student who communicates a great deal is likely to become aroused and upset by unfavorable social comparisons that inevitably result from frequent communication. One of our findings was that students were ambivalent about communication; many had approach-avoidance conflicts. Often behavior that would be useful from a coping point of view presented distinct problems of defense. Students who were most central in the communication structure, especially those in the second-year group, were those who were most anxious. The relationship between rates of communication and anxiety, however, was not a simple one. Students who felt that they needed guidance about how to prepare for examinations saw communication with other students as a necessary tool for coping. These students sought out others to learn how they were preparing. The students who were fairly anxious—who became even more so in talking with other students who seemed better organized than they—then would withdraw from communication. The problem they faced was whether to pursue information that might add to their efficacy in coping or to avoid communication and, hence, increased anxiety. In short, the student seemed to fluctuate from time to time in his communication patterns, depending on his anxiety level. Some balance was attempted between dealing with coping and defense needs.

As we have shown, communication did serve at times to meet defense needs. The student who needed reassurance would seek support and validation for comforting beliefs. To the extent that such support could be obtained, he could regard his views with confidence. But, since communication could lead to both comfort and discomfort, students often communicated with caution. Furthermore, much of the communication, as examinations approached, was especially concerned with defense needs, while students avoided discussing materials that could possibly arouse anxiety.

As we have attempted to point out, it is difficult to determine the functional ability of a coping or defense device, since both short-run and long-range consequences must be understood. Moreover, the relationships between coping and defense devices are not simple. What may be extremely functional, speaking in terms of the defense system, may be very restricting from the point of view of active coping. If both systems are considered simultaneously, it is obvious that when a device is functional for both systems at the same point in time it is most functional for the person. Mastery of difficult material, for example, can serve both coping and defense needs.

The students' moods and fluctuations in moods seemed clearly associated with environmental factors. Whereas favorable mood changes were experienced after active mastery of material and indications of adequate adaptation, depressive moods were encountered when adaptive attempts seemed to be failing. One of the most common contingencies of unpleasant mood states was unfavorable social comparison or some clear indications of adaptive failures. This led to self-doubt, questioning of motives and abilities, and further served to handicap coping attempts (concentration, study, and the like).

Time sequence also played an important part in making an adequate adaptive response. The student who reassured himself too early and too easily ran the risk of harnessing effective motivation to expend coping efforts. Thus the student who defended himself against anxiety too early by avoiding discussion of examinations lost possible benefits from such discussions. Defense was important, but the student who exposed himself and protected himself only when exposure had little further gain was able to utilize his coping and defense capabilities in a consistent, congruent fashion.

The dimensions of stress situations are likely to be important in determining what adaptive devices are most efficacious. The person under stress must gauge his preparation in terms of what he perceives as the duration of the situation. Pacing thus becomes an important adaptive technique. There are indications, for example, that lack of knowledge of the duration of a stress situation can clearly make it more difficult to achieve a proper adaptive response. Farber,[3] in a study of prisoners, demonstrated that the prisoners who suffered most were those with indeterminate sentences. These men, not knowing whether to become strongly identified with the prison group or to maintain their outside reference groups, consequently were limited and less effective in their responses.

But merely knowing the duration of a situation does not insure adequate response. Most of the students under study knew the duration of their situations, yet, as examinations approached, they had to abandon early plans as

3. M. L. Farber, "Suffering and Time Perspective of the Prisoner," *Univ. Iowa Stud. Child Welf., 20,* 1944, 153-227.

unrealistic and revise their studying approaches. Many students, failing to pace themselves correctly, reached a stage of study exhaustion at the point where effective studying would have been valuable. Others started studying too late and failed even to approximate their anticipated plans.

This study, largely a descriptive one, has attempted to show how a group of students went about dealing with a "threat" situation of considerable importance. We must remember, however, that this situation is qualitatively different from other types of threat situations. A variety of similar descriptive studies still remains necessary in varying contexts. For example, in this study social comparison was an important phenomenon in part because no clear standard existed that students could use to gauge their abilities and progress. In academic departments with more clearly defined realms of knowledge, it is likely that social comparison and communication would play a lesser role. We would expect less social comparison, for example, in a department of mathematics than in a department of sociology. In this instance, however, because there was no clear standard in the department studied, other students were used as a means of evaluating one's own standing. In future studies it will also be important to consider the effects of varying other dimensions of stress situations.

Although qualitatively different from many other stress situations, we have pointed out the many similarities in response to stress between the students under study and combat troops studied by Grinker and Spiegel. This is probably indicative that some of the reactions we observed are more general responses to long-term stresses. These include comforting cognitions, drawing on past experience, identification with others undergoing similar experiences, joking, avoidance, hostility, magical-type thinking, and creating a favorable picture of the future. Also both the students under study and combat soldiers were faced with learning exactly what stimuli interfered with adequate adaptation and how to deal with them. As Grinker and Spiegel pointed out:

This is an actual learning process. The situation may appear at first to be innocuous and the primary reaction to combat is usually detachment and objective interest. The antiaircraft fire may look like a spectacular but harmless Fourth of July celebration, entertaining but not dangerous. The attitude is soon changed by the repeated demonstration of the destructive effectiveness of flak bursts. Other possible dangers are only appreciated after some objective demonstration has alerted the ego. After a crash due to motor failure, the most vigorous attention may be paid to the sound of the motors, a sound which was never given any special emphasis before. Sounds, sudden flashes of light, and other physical phenomena may become so intimately associated with a dangerous meaning that the interpretation becomes automatic and involuntary.[4]

In a similar fashion the students under study became aware of the situations that evoked their anxiety. If they did not studiously avoid these situations, they at least did begin to more carefully edit their behavior and control their reactions by various defensive devices in these situations. Thus they would continue to communicate but use joking to avoid serious discussion, or more carefully select those with whom they communicated.

Earlier we pointed out that as compared with a short stress situation studied by Hamburg and Associates, the "ace in the hole" or "I don't give a damn" reaction was relatively unsuccessful in the long duration stress situation. It is particularly interesting that Grinker and Spiegel also reported that the "I don't give a damn" reaction was not particularly effective in the combat situation:

---

4. Grinker and Spiegel, *op. cit.,* p. 127.

The "I don't give a damn" reaction is actually closer to a masked depression than to a successful adaptation, but it does protect the individual against anxiety. The protection, however, is unstable and often breaks down when the individual comes close to the end of his combat tour. The reaction is most often seen when combat losses are very high and the mathematical chances for survival very low. During the last few missions, hope of survival once more becomes realistic, and at that point concern for his own fate again returns to the individual. Once he begins to hope and to care, he may suddenly develop intense anxiety.[5]

More successful among both the students under study and combat troops was the comforting cognition that "It can't happen to me." A number of the students found various justifications for the attitude that they would be passed even if they performed poorly, and this attitude served to reduce anxiety. Unfortunately, combat troops found their feelings of invulnerability shattered as a result of experiencing "near-hits" and seeing close associates killed.[6]

What we have attempted to present is a rough paradigm for the study of stress situations. We have argued that the source of stress and failure at adaptation may be dependent on the person—his abilities and capabilities, on the group—the tools and techniques it provides for adaptation, and on the situation itself—the exigencies that must be dealt with.

An adequate culture and tradition teach the young how to deal with environmental exigencies, and an adequate person learns effectively how to do this. The magnitude of stress is dependent upon the extent of imbalance between

5. *Ibid.*, p. 132.

6. I. L. Janis, *Air War and Emotional Stress* (New York: McGraw-Hill Book Co., Inc., 1951); and Martha Wolfenstein, *Disaster: A Psychological Essay* (New York: The Free Press of Glencoe, 1957).

the group's environment and the patterns available for dealing with the environment. When imbalances exist between environmental problems and cultural and social resources, we have what we might call "stress situations inherent within the cultural and social systems." The nature of these stress situations may be amplified by sociological analysis.

In this study, we have centered on social psychological problems in adaptation. In brief we have attempted to show how the group may be viewed as a major influence in understanding adaptive processes. And, since one of the most fascinating facets of human behavior is the marvelous persistence and adaptability of man in an environment of changing circumstances, varied demands, and difficult challenges, perhaps the most important question we can ask about human behavior is how man continues to persist and maintain "health" and "balance" in the complex circumstances of modern life.

BIBLIOGRAPHY

Alexander, F. *Psychosomatic Medicine: Its Principles and Applications.* New York: W. W. Norton and Co., 1950.

Allport, G. W. *The Nature of Prejudice.* Cambridge: Addison-Wesley, 1954.

Bales, Robert. *Interaction Process Analysis.* Cambridge: Addison-Wesley, 1950.

Basowitz, H., Persky, H., Korchin, S. J., and Grinker, R. R. *Anxiety and Stress.* New York: McGraw-Hill, 1955.

Bettelheim, B. "Individual and Mass Behavior in Extreme Situations," *J. Abnorm. Soc. Psychol., 38,* 1943, 417-452.

Bondy, C. "Problems of Internment Camps," *J. Abnorm. Soc. Psychol., 38,* 1943, 453-475.

Brewster, H. H. "Separation Reaction in Psychosomatic Disease and Neurosis," *Psychosomatic Medicine, 14,* 1952, 154-160.

Caudill, W. "Cultural Perspectives on Stress," *Symposium on Stress.* Washington: National Research Council and Walter Reed Army Medical Center, 1953.

————. "Effects of Social and Cultural Systems in Reactions to Stress," *Memorandum to the Committee on Preventive Medicine and Social Research.* New York: Social Science Research Council, 1958.

Clinard, Marshall. *Sociology of Deviant Behavior.* New York: Holt, Rinehart & Winston, 1957.

Cohen, Albert K. *Delinquent Boys, The Culture of the Gang.* New York: The Free Press of Glencoe, 1955.

Cohen, E. A. *Human Behavior in the Concentration Camp.* New York: W. W. Norton and Co., 1953.

Coser, Rose L. "Some Social Functions of Laughter," *Human Relations, 12,* 1959, 171-182.

Davis, K. *Human Society.* New York: Macmillan, 1949.

Dollard, J., Doob, L., Miller, N., Mowrer, O., and Sears, R. *Frustration and Aggression.* New Haven: Yale University Press, 1939.

222

Dunbar, H. F. *Emotions and Bodily Changes*. New York: Columbia University Press, 1954.

_____. *Psychosomatic Diagnosis*. New York: Paul B. Hoeber, 1945.

Farber, M. L. "Suffering and Time Perspective of the Prisoner," *Univ. Iowa Stud. Child Welf., 20,* 1944, 153-227.

Festinger, Leon. *A Theory of Cognitive Dissonance*. Evanston: Row, Peterson and Company, 1957.

_____. "A Theory of Social Comparison Processes," in Hare, P., Borgatta, E. F., and Bales, R. F., *Small Groups*. New York: Alfred A. Knopf, 1955.

Fox, Renée. *Experiment Perilous*. New York: The Free Press of Glencoe, 1959.

French, J. R. P., Jr. "Organized and Unorganized Groups Under Fear and Frustration," *Univ. Iowa Stud. Child Welf., 20,* 1944, 229-308.

Funkenstein, D. H., King, S. H., and Drolette, M. E. *Mastery of Stress*. Cambridge: Harvard University Press, 1957.

Goffman, E. *The Presentation of Self in Everyday Life*. Garden City: Doubleday Anchor, 1959.

Grinker, R. R. *Psychosomatic Research*. New York: W. W. Norton and Co., 1953.

_____, and Spiegel, J. P. *Men Under Stress*. New York: McGraw-Hill Book Co., Inc., 1945.

Hall, C. S., and Lindzey, G. *Theories of Personality*. New York: John Wiley and Sons, Inc., 1957.

Halliday, J. L. *Psychosocial Medicine: A Study of the Sick Society*. New York: W. W. Norton and Co., 1948.

Hamburg, D. "Psychological Adaptive Processes in Life-Threatening Injuries," in *Symposium on Stress*. Washington: National Research Council and Walter Reed Army Medical Center, 1953.

_____, Hamburg, B., and deGoza, S. "Adaptive Problems and Mechanisms in Severely Burned Patients," *Psychiatry, 16,* 1953, 1-20.

Hamilton, M. *Psychosomatics*. New York: John Wiley, 1955.

Hare, P., Borgatta, E. F., and Bales, R. F. *Small Groups*. New York: Alfred A. Knopf, 1955.

Hayner, N., and Ash, E. "The Prison as a Community," *American Sociological Review, 5,* 1940, 577-583.

Heron, W. "The Pathology of Boredom," *Scientific American,*
196, 1957, 52-56.

Hinkle, L. E., Jr., and Plummer, N. "Life Stress and Industrial Absenteeism," *Industrial Medicine and Surgery,*
21, 1952, 363-375.

————, and Wolff, H. G. "Health and the Social Environ-
ment: Experimental Investigations," in Leighton, A. H.,
Clausen, J. A., and Wilson, R. N. (eds.), *Explorations in
Social Psychiatry.* New York: Basic, 1957.

Hollingshead, A. B., and Redlich, F. C. *Social Class and
Mental Illness.* New York: John Wiley, 1958.

Jaco, E. G. (ed.). *Patients, Physicians and Illness.* New York:
The Free Press of Glencoe, 1958.

Janis, I. L. *Air War and Emotional Stress.* New York:
McGraw-Hill Book Co., Inc., 1951.

————. *Psychological Stress.* New York: John Wiley, 1958.

Kaplan, Howard B., and Bloom, Samuel W. "The Use of
Sociological and Social-Psychological Concepts in Physio-
logical Research," *The Journal of Nervous and Mental
Disease, 131,* 1960, 128-134.

Leighton, A. H., Clausen, J. A., and Wilson, R. N. (eds.).
Explorations in Social Psychiatry. New York: Basic, 1957.

Lewin, K. *Resolving Social Conflicts.* New York: Harper, 1948.

Liebman, S. (ed.). *Stress Situations.* Philadelphia: J. B. Lippincott Co., 1955.

Lindemann, E. "Modifications in the Course of Ulcerative
Colitis in Relationship to Changes in Life Situations and
Reaction Patterns," in Res. Publ. Assn. Nerv. Ment. Dis.,
29, *Life Stress and Bodily Disease.* Baltimore: Williams
and Wilkins, 1950, 706-723.

Mechanic, D. "Illness and Social Disability: Some Problems
in Analysis," *Pacific Sociological Review, 2,* 1959, 37-41.

————, and Volkart, E. H. "Illness Behavior and Medical
Diagnoses," *Journal of Health and Human Behavior, 1,*
1960, 86-94.

————, and ————. "Stress, Illness Behavior and the Sick
Role," *American Sociological Review, 26,* 1961, 51-58.

Merton, R. K. *Social Theory and Social Structure.* New York:
The Free Press of Glencoe, 1957.

Munroe, Ruth L. *Schools of Psychoanalytic Thought.* New
York: Dryden Press, 1955.

Parsons, Talcott. *The Social System.* New York: The Free Press of Glencoe, 1951.

Pepitone, A. "Motivational Effects in Social Perception," *Human Relations, 3,* 1950, 57-76.

Postman, L., and Bruner, J. S. "Perception Under Stress," *Psychol. Rev., 55,* 1948, 314-323.

Res. Publ. Assn. Nerv. Ment. Dis., *29, Life Stress and Bodily Disease.* Baltimore: Williams and Wilkins, 1950.

Ruesch, J. "Social Technique, Social Status and Social Change in Illness," in Kluckhohn, C., and Murray, H. (eds.), *Personality in Nature, Society and Culture.* New York: Alfred A. Knopf, 1948.

————, and Bateson, G. *Communication: The Social Matrix of Psychiatry.* New York: W. W. Norton and Co., 1951.

Schachter, S., and Burdick, H. A. "A Field Experiment on Rumor Transmission and Distortion," *J. Abnorm. Soc. Psychol., 50,* 1955, 363-371.

Schein, E. H. "Some Observations on Chinese Methods of Handling Prisoners of War," *Public Opinion Quarterly, 20,* 1956, 321-327.

————. "The Chinese Indoctrination Program for Prisoners of War," *Psychiatry, 19,* 1956, 149-172.

Selye, H. *The Stress of Life.* New York: McGraw-Hill, 1956.

Sherif, M., and Cantril, H. *The Psychology of Ego-Involvements.* New York: John Wiley and Sons, Inc., 1947.

Simmons, L., and Wolff, H. G. *Social Science in Medicine.* New York: Russell Sage Foundation, 1954.

Simpson, G. E., and Yinger, J. M. *Racial and Cultural Minorities.* New York: Harper and Bros., 1953.

Smock, C. D. "The Relationship between Test Anxiety, 'Threat-Expectancy' and Recognition Thresholds for Words," *Journal of Personality, 25,* 1956, 191-201.

Sullivan, A. J., and McKell, T. E. *Personality in Peptic Ulcer.* Springfield: Charles C Thomas, 1950.

Sullivan, H. S. *Conceptions of Modern Psychiatry.* Washington: The William Alanson White Psychiatric Foundation, 1947.

————. "Psychiatry: Introduction to the Study of Interpersonal Relations," *Psychiatry, 1,* 1938, 121-134.

————. *The Interpersonal Theory of Psychiatry.* New York: W. W. Norton and Co., 1953.

Sykes, G., and Messinger, S. "The Inmate Social System," in *Theoretical Studies in Social Organization of the Prison.* New York: Social Science Research Council, 1960.

Symposium on Stress. Washington: National Research Council and Walter Reed Army Medical Center, 1953.

Thibaut, J., and Kelley, H. H. *The Social Psychology of Groups.* New York: John Wiley and Sons, Inc., 1959.

Toby, Jackson. "Some Variables in Role Conflict Analysis," *Social Forces, 30,* 1952, 323-327.

Volkart, E. H. "Bereavement and Mental Health," in Leighton, A. H., Clausen, J. A., and Wilson, R. N. (eds.). *Explorations in Social Psychiatry.* New York: Basic, 1957.

_____ (ed.). *Social Behavior and Personality.* New York: Social Science Research Council, 1951.

Weber, Max. *The Methodology of the Social Sciences.* New York: The Free Press of Glencoe, 1949.

Weider, A. (ed.). *Contributions Toward Medical Psychology,* Vol. I. New York: Ronald Press Co., 1953.

Weiss, E., and English, O. S. *Psychosomatic Medicine.* Philadelphia: W. B. Saunders, 1943.

Wolf, S., and Wolff, H. G. *Human Gastric Function: An Experimental Study of a Man and His Stomach.* New York: Oxford University Press, 1943.

Wolfenstein, Martha. *Disaster: A Psychological Essay.* New York: The Free Press of Glencoe, 1957.

Wolff, H. G. "Disease and the Patterns of Behavior," in Jaco, E. G. (ed.), *Patients, Physicians and Illness.* New York: The Free Press of Glencoe, 1958.

_____. "Life Situations, Emotions and Bodily Disease," in *Symposium on Stress.* Washington: National Research Council and Walter Reed Army Medical Center, 1953.

_____. "Stress and Adaptive Patterns Resulting in Tissue Damage in Man," in *The Medical Clinics of North America.* Philadelphia: W. B. Saunders, 1955.

_____. *Stress and Disease.* Springfield: Charles C Thomas, 1953.

_____. "Stress, Emotions and Bodily Disease," in Galdston, I. (ed.). *Medicine and Science.* New York: International Universities Press, 1954.

INDEX